UConn's Dream Season

UConn's Dream Season

Road to the Final Eight

George Ferencz, Jr.
and
David P. Tosatti

Bonus Books, Inc., Chicago

94 93 92 91 90   5 4 3 2 1

Library of Congress Catalog Card Number: 90-83767

International Standard Book Number: 0-929387-49-X

Bonus Books, Inc.
160 East Illinois Street
Chicago, Illinois 60611

First Edition

Printed in the United States of America

Unless otherwise noted, all photographs are courtesy of *Daily Campus* archives.

To my parents, my brother, my grandparents, my family, and all my friends for their support all of these years. I couldn't have done it without you. Also, in memory of a good friend, Robert Hutchinson.

—G.F.

To my father.

—D.T.

Contents

Acknowledgments

Reliving one of the greatest moments in University of Connecticut sports history was a pleasure. When looking back on UConn's 1989–90 basketball season, one can not help but get goose bumps when remembering Tate George's last-second shot against Clemson or John Gwynn ecstatically snipping the nets down in Madison Square Garden after the Huskies won the Big East tournament. These moments are frozen in not only our memories but the memories of every UConn fan. The season was a true testament to the devotion of the Connecticut fan. To that end, we both acknowledge the players and coaching staff of the 1989–90 UConn basketball team and the Husky fans for the memories they provided the state.

We also must thank those whose guidance was immeasurable in this project. First, the entire Sports Information Department at the University of Connecticut deserves thanks for their aid throughout the year, especially Associate Athletic Director Tim Tolokan who helped us keep our facts straight during this project. Others whose time and effort do not go unappreciated are Peter Gammons of ESPN, Bryant Thomas and Bob Steele of WTIC, and Gil Santos of the Big East Network.

We especially wish to thank Coach Jim Calhoun for his help. Others who dealt with us during this project and deserve some special recognition are C.J. Gunther, Lois McLean, Jason Kauppi, Catherine Keating, and Amy Seligman. We thank Owen Hurd and the people at Bonus Books. Also, thanks to journalism professor John Breen. Without him we could not have written this book. Thanks for getting us started.

I would like to thank Mom, Dad, Bryan, and the rest of my family for all the support they have given me through the years. Those efforts will never be forgotten, and will always be appreciated.

George Ferencz, Jr.
August 1990

For the people responsible for getting me where I am, I thank you. None of this would have taken place without my family's support and interest. Thanks Mom, Dad, and Mags. To the Groton School community for allowing me to experience what that place is like, I send immeasurable thanks. And to my father, who taught me the thrill of competition and the love of sport, I am forever indebted. There is no other person whose practices I would rather emulate or whose values I deem higher. My portion of this book is for him and the efforts of the GST Foundation.

David P. Tosatti
August 1990

Foreword

There are many joys and sorrows in sports. Jim Calhoun's 1989–90 Connecticut season was a mirror of the joys and sorrows of college basketball.

UConn's slow, stumbling start in the Big East season reached its lowest point after a 31-point hammering at the hands of St. John's. This loss dropped the Huskies conference record to 0–2. Despite playing well and winning nine games against outside opposition early in the season, the thought was that perhaps UConn would be hard-pressed to do much in the very fast company of the Big East.

All that changed the night of January 15, 1990, at the Hartford Civic Center when UConn upset Syracuse. Lightning struck again in the same spot a few nights later when the Huskies beat Georgetown.

I broadcast the UConn-Syracuse game on the Big East television network and remember remarking to Big East Commissioner Dave Gavitt that I was very impressed with the totally unselfish style of UConn's play. I could not help but think that they played the game of basketball with intelligence. Week after week and upset after upset, they displayed the same kind of work ethic and selfless style of play that had characterized the Celtics championship teams I covered throughout the 1980s.

The 1989–90 Huskies had players that would pass up a ten-foot shot, make the extra pass, and get a six-footer for a teammate. They were playing basketball the way I believe the game was meant to be played—five individuals working together as a unit on offense and defense toward one common goal: to win.

Of course, Connecticut's last two games in the NCAA tournament had all the emotional ups and downs of some of their entire seasons in recent years. Tate Goerge's unforgettable shot to beat Clemson at the buzzer put them one step away from the Final Four. Then Christian Laettner's last-second shot sent the Huskies home. A tough way to end a game, a season, a dream.

But the UConn Huskies should take solace in the fact that they played the game of basketball the way it was meant to be played: with teamwork, tough defense, and lots of heart. They indeed lived up to the words of immortal sports-writer, Grant Rice, "When the great scorer comes to mark against your name, he'll not put 'won' or 'lost,' but how you played the game."

Gil Santos
Big East Television Network
September 1990

Introduction

There had to be a hollowness inside every UConn basketball fan. Whether they were sitting, standing, or kneeling in prayer, they had to believe all the magic was spent. What a terrific ride it had been. Their Huskies had won a school-record thirty games and lost just five, even though defeat number six appeared just one second away. UConn had swept the Big East like a tornado, winning the regular-season crown and, in the span of less than fifty-four hours, defeating Seton Hall, Georgetown, and Syracuse to win its first-ever Big East championship.

The Huskies subsequently earned the top seed in the NCAA East Regional. UConn had not even been invited to the NCAA tournament since 1979. And in their home away from home, the Hartford Civic Center, the Huskies dismissed their first two opponents, Boston University and California, in convincing fashion. UConn's next stop was East Rutherford, New Jersey, for a regional semifinal date with Clemson. Through most of the game UConn dominated, but David Young hit a three-point shot with 11.3 seconds left to give Clemson a 70–69 lead.

Tate George took the in-bounds pass and moved the ball up the court, taking the fate of the contest into his own hands. George's jumper from near the top of the key was no good. Clemson's Sean Tyson grabbed the rebound and was fouled immediately. But he missed the front end on the one-and-one and the Huskies got the rebound. They called time-out just before the buzzer could sound. The clock read, "00:01."

"One second . . . what could possibly happen in that span of time? Might as well just end the game," most UConn fans must have been thinking. This one second would tell a lot, about the fans and the team.

The team was a young one. Sophomore Chris Smith had been UConn's leading scorer throughout the season. Nadav Henefeld, a twenty-one-year-old freshman from Israel, had proved he had one of the most well-rounded games in the Big East Conference. Which one would take the last desperation heave? What kind of shot would it be? UConn had to take the ball the entire length of the court and then shoot. As soon as the ball was touched in bounds, the clock would start.

Throughout the year, no one UConn player dominated games from start to finish. Individual efforts keyed this team, and toward the end of each game one or two Huskies would step into the spotlight. Now the Huskies really needed a miracle worker.

Scott Burrell, a freshman from Hamden, Connecticut, took the ball at the baseline following two timeouts. He looked down the entire length of the court. There were ninety-four feet between him and his teammates. The Huskies were lucky Burrell was with them this season. The freshman's speed and agility helped execute the press defense, and he was equally capable on the offensive end. Burrell, though, almost never became a Husky. The Seattle Mariners offered Burrell, a well-recruited pitcher, a contract in excess of $100,000 to join their system.

Tate George was the captain of this team. He had survived the 9–19 freshman season, had been there when UConn won the NIT, and now was on the court in perhaps the most critical moment in UConn basketball history. George helped the team form a solid mold. Coach Jim Calhoun had been known to give George a few tongue-lashings, but only to make George a better basketball player. It was like a drill sergeant preparing his troops for battle. This moment, with one lonely tick left on the clock, was the heat of battle.

Burrell took the ball from the referee, and cocked his arm as though he was going to fire a fastball. The ball sailed through the air and the UConn fans who could bare to look watched it descend. The ball was headed for George. Burrell had thrown many strikes in his career, but surely none more accurate than this one. The 6'5" George reached up and came down with the ball. George spun toward the basket and Clemson's Sean Tyson backed away, arms partially in the air. George jumped, shot, and . . .

On Wednesday, March 22, 1989, the University of Connecticut basketball team purposefully strode onto its home court. The goal: sustain a twenty-six-game winning streak in Storrs and advance to the National Invitation Tournament's final four. The 18-12 Huskies, playing in front of 4,604 partisan fans, were hoping to re-create the pandemonium of 1988, when they defeated Ohio State, 72-67, for the NIT championship.

By night's end, UConn had relinquished the crown it wore proudly for 357 days. After Alabama-Birmingham's 85-79 victory, questions were raised by the Husky faithful. Could the program again reach the same heights it had in winning the NIT? Would UConn rebound from this loss and make a run at the 1990 NCAA tournament? Was the NIT championship just a brief shining moment in a series of mediocre seasons?

The disappointment was fueled by the high expectations UConn fans brought into 1988-89. At the season's outset, UConn sought to end an eleven-year absence from the NCAA tournament. Hopes were high: the Huskies had 84 percent of their offensive output—and all their starters—back from the NIT title team. And in Chris Smith, they were adding the number-one high school player in the state.

Leading the way was Cliff Robinson, who would average 20.0 points and 7.4 rebounds during 1988-89. Also back was guard Phil Gamble, a fine scorer who was voted the most outstanding player in the 1988 NIT. The Big East coaches picked the Huskies to finish fourth in the conference. And after UConn opened the season with victories over Hartford, Yale, and Marist, the team was ranked eighteenth nationally by the Associated Press.

The Huskies dropped out of the Top Twenty following an 88-73 loss at Purdue but rebounded with a victory at Virginia. UConn then won its next five games, including a defeat of Villanova in the Big East opener. After that the Huskies went 5-10 in conference play and finished seventh. A loss to eventual national runner-up Seton Hall in the Big East tournament quarterfinals dashed their hopes of being invited to the NCAA dance. Then came the NIT disappointment, and UConn fans were left to wonder

John Gwynn drives in for a layup against Standard Oil, only to have his shot rejected by former Husky Jeff King.

Entering the 1989–90 pre-season, Coach Calhoun's main concern was how to mix the youth and experience on his team into a squad that could compete in the Big East Conference. Gone were Robinson, Gamble, and Willie McCloud, and with them a majority of UConn's 1988–89 points. But their departure also marked the end of the Dom Perno era at UConn. Perno, head coach at UConn for nine seasons, had been replaced after the Huskies finished 12–16 in 1985–86.

In came Jim Calhoun. In his first season, 1986–87, the Huskies went 9–19; the next year brought the NIT championship and a 20–14 record. The 1988–89 campaign, though ending at a respectable 18–13 mark, was considered a step backward when the Huskies fell short of successfully defending their NIT title. So for Calhoun and his young squad, there was no better way to test the waters than with pre-season battles against Marathon Oil (a semi-pro club) and the Soviet National Team.

Lyman DePriest threads his way through a crowded lane.

where the program was headed.

There was some promise for 1989–90. Smith had started seventeen games and averaged 9.9 points as a freshman. Also back was Tate George, the team's only senior and a co-captain, who had dished out 152 assists the previous year. Coach Jim Calhoun's other returnees included juniors John Gwynn, Lyman DePriest, co-captain Steve Pikiell, and Murray Williams, and sophomores Rod Sellers, Dan Cyrulik, Tim Pikiell, and Marc Suhr. The newcomers were Toraino Walker, Scott Burrell, Oliver Macklin, Marte Smith, and Nadav Henefeld.

These fifteen players held the hopes of the UConn faithful who felt unfulfilled after the 1988–89 season. Even the most optimistic fans could not have guessed what this young group would accomplish under the glare of the national spotlight.

Chapter 1

Starting Over, Starting Young
November 1, 1989

Chris Smith was one player Calhoun would depend on for high point production. His 31 points led the team in the opening victory.

Oddly enough, or perhaps not, the Marathon Oil team had several UConn alumni on its roster. Willie McCloud, Jeff King, and Phil Gamble—all members of the Marathon Oil club—made the Huskies' first exhibition game look more like an alumni match than a tune-up for a Big East season.

After just two weeks of practice, Calhoun got the opportunity to answer some questions that were surrounding the team in the pre-season. For instance, which players would fill the scoring gap left by departed seniors Robinson, Gamble, and McCloud, who had accounted for 51 percent of the Huskies' 1988–89 scoring? The answer, at least in the Marathon Oil game, came in a 6'2" package called Chris Smith.

"Smitty" tallied 31 points in just twenty-seven minutes, sinking 12 of 20 from the floor with five of the baskets from three-point range. His efforts helped the Huskies to a 101–78 victory and suggested that Calhoun's installation of a perimeter offense to compensate for the loss of Robinson in the middle was indeed prudent. The Huskies took twenty-four three-point shots in the game.

In Smith, Calhoun had found his primary scorer. Nadav Henefeld, the 6'7" former Israeli soldier, also showed he would be an integral part of the new-look Huskies.

With UConn trailing 18–11 early in the first half, Marathon Oil's King took a feed from Gamble on a fast break and jammed it in to extend their lead to nine. Shortly thereafter UConn cut the lead to three, and then one of the new breed of Huskies made his debut. In his first play on the court, Henefeld threaded the needle to Smith on a drive to cut Marathon's lead to 31–30. A minute later, with the score 33–31, Henefeld showed his international style of play as he blocked a shot at one end of the court, raced down to the other end, took a feed from Smith, and sank the game-tying layup. Henefeld

One of four candidates for the center position at the start of the season, Dan Cyrulik posts up against one of Standard's big men.

fastball, was drafted out of Hamden High by the Seattle Mariners. But he would turn down a $100,000-plus contract, and instead heed the words of his brother, Abbott Burrell (a tri-captain of the 1989 UConn football squad), and go to college. Scott Burrell, the basketball player, brought the flash aspect to the Huskies as he took an alley-oop pass from Tate George and slammed it home. Burrell finished with just 4 points, but he also chipped in 4 assists and grabbed 6 rebounds as a starter in his first college game.

Concern in the middle forced Calhoun to test four different players at the center position. Dan Cyrulik played sparingly in the contest. The 7'1" sophomore from Williamsville, New York, would have to wait a little longer to get into the spotlight. After a redshirt year, Marc Suhr, the 7'1½" sophomore from Cologne, West Germany, contributed 8 points and 3 rebounds. Another prospect in the middle was Toraino Walker of Orlando, Florida. The muscular 6'6" freshman figured to play power forward, but he was adept at using his big body to clear out the middle.

Rod Sellers was originally expected to fill the shoes of Robinson, who was drafted in the second round by the Portland Trail Blazers. The 6'9" sophomore from Florence, South Carolina, had spent 1988–89 practicing against Robinson. Against Marathon, Sellers would collect 12 rebounds, including 7 on the offensive boards, and score 9 points in twenty-two minutes of action. But Sellers had not totally matured as a center, and Calhoun was determined to get the offensive reliance of the team away from the center position.

After leading by three at the half, 48–45, UConn went on a 7–0 run thanks to a three-point play by Smith, and field goals by George and Sellers. UConn extended its lead to 84–70 with 4:42 left in the game when George buried a three. Then Burrell's alley-oop slam, followed by a George steal and a Smith three-pointer, put the game out of reach with 3:38 to go. It was the Connecticut fans' first look at the Huskies' running offense—a rarity in the days of Robinson. The fast-paced style was more the way Calhoun's teams at Northeastern moved the ball.

The responsibility of controlling this sort of

finished with 8 points and 3 rebounds in just eight minutes of work.

Henefeld was not the only newcomer to grab the fans' attention. Scott Burrell looked to make some noise during his debut. Burrell, an outstanding baseball pitcher with a 90 m.p.h.-plus

Gwynn (15) the "mini-microwave," leads a breakaway against Phil Gamble (12) and Eric Turner (14). DePriest (23) is flared out on his right.

tempo fell not only with Smith, but also with the veteran George. George entered the season with 823 career points and 498 assists; 36 assists shy of Karl Hobbs' school record. As the lone senior on the club, and the only UConn player to be coached by Calhoun for four straight seasons, George's role as team leader was magnified. The leadership qualities expected of him went beyond the number of points he could put on the scoreboard. Indeed, Calhoun looked for George to guide the younger members of the squad in intangible ways—through work ethic and spirit as well as talent.

George's co-captain title went beyond name alone. He became the symbol of Connecticut pride during a year in which there was no single superstar. In both games and practices, George stepped out and took charge of a team needing some veteran leadership. Against Marathon Oil, George had 16 points and 9 assists. He smoothly ran the UConn attack during a time when Calhoun most needed to see everyone's offensive capabilities.

The backcourt of Smith and George earned praise prior to the start of the season as one of the most potent tandems in the nation. The flashy sophomore, who could do so much with the basketball, and his partner, the experienced senior, both said that in order to have a successful year they would have to rely on one another on the court. True to their predictions, their guard play became the cornerstone of the UConn team.

John Gwynn might have been just six feet tall, but that did not stop him from driving to the basket. Calhoun started the feisty junior against Marathon Oil, and Gwynn responded with 13 points, 6 of 8 from the floor. Still, Gwynn had to realize that Smith and George would be the one-two punch for the Huskies. Like the 1988–89 season, when he averaged 10.4 minutes a game and 5.6 points, Gwynn would end up being UConn's sixth man. His role was to come off the bench and give the Huskies a spark when they needed it most. Gwynn's production off the bench earned him the nickname "mini-microwave," after the NBA champion Detroit Pistons guard Vinnie "Microwave" Johnson. The Huskies hoped that like Johnson, Gwynn's hot flashes off the bench could lead them to a championship.

Also returning in the backcourt was co-captain Steve Pikiell. Pikiell, who entered UConn the same year as George, was making his

The Huskies played solid defense, holding Standard Oil to 42 percent shooting and forcing 17 turnovers.

UConn also did a good job of hitting the boards, outrebounding the taller Standard Oil team. Rod Sellers (22) led the Huskies with 12 boards.

first on-court appearance since the NIT title season. After sitting out 1988–89 with an injured shoulder, Pikiell was back and ready to supply the off-court leadership the Huskies needed to complete the squad.

As Calhoun's Huskies left the court with the 101–78 victory, they left behind them the UConn basketball past. King and McCloud left to pursue their individual interests, while Phil Gamble returned to the university to complete work on his bachelor's degree.

Calhoun said goodbye to the past that night. The Perno era was over: no longer could the Huskies depend on the inside play of their departed big men. The 1989–90 version of the Huskies had arrived. The elements for success were there: an excellent guard trio, a fine outside shooter, and a few big bodies. What UConn needed to formulate was a high caliber Big East defense that could shut down the likes of Alonzo Mourning, Derrick Coleman, Brian Shorter, and Greg "Boo" Harvey. The past was left behind, the present was at hand, and a glimpse at the future was to come in just twelve days.

Chapter 2

Foreign Diplomacy,
Husky Style
November 13, 1989

A crowd of just over 12,500 welcomed the Huskies for the first game of the 1989–90 season at the Hartford Civic Center. In the spirit of *glasnost,* the fans also greeted the national team from the Soviet Union with open arms. Pregame gifts were exchanged as the teams lined up at center court. Once the traditional goodwill ceremonies were over, UConn was set to concentrate on the game at hand. The less-than-capacity crowd did not lack in enthusiasm, as they waited for their Huskies to give them something to cheer about. Why did approximately 3,500 stay away from this game? Possibly because it was a pre-season match, or maybe it was that the Huskies were not even playing an NCAA opponent. Whatever the reason, those who witnessed UConn's 97–87 victory over the Soviet National Team might claim they saw the future of Connecticut basketball that night.

The Soviet Nationals came into Hartford fresh off five-point losses to the nation's top two ranked teams, Nevada-Las Vegas and Louisiana State. But the Soviets scored more than 100 points in both games, and that may have caused

feelings of uneasiness in UConn fans. There were questions about the young team's ability to defeat a team that played so well against the top two teams in the nation. This experienced Soviet team also had defeated the United States in the 1988 Seoul Olympics.

Even Calhoun had doubts about how his team would handle the Soviet attack. "The expectations of me personally were if we could be competitive, the kids would be satisfied in the sense that it's progress," he said. Calling the Soviets better than Big East teams, Calhoun added that his Huskies might not be capable of playing at that level so early in the season.

Calhoun considered doing what was thought to be the impossible. "They say you can't press the Russians," he said, but his team would try to prove otherwise. In an attempt to stay competitive with the Soviet National team, Calhoun instituted the press that had made him a winning coach at Northeastern. In turn, the Soviets were held to just 37 percent shooting from the floor, compared to 54 percent shooting against LSU and 45 percent against UNLV. Even from three-point range, where the Soviets previously shot 49 percent, they could muster just 7 of 19 (.368). Calhoun's gamble had paid off.

Though UConn's defense led the way to victory, the Huskies' offense played a vital role as well. Chris Smith scored 28 points against a taller Soviet squad. Smith's position in the lineup, and in Calhoun's running game, seemed secure. What still remained a mystery was how to fill the void in the middle. Rod Sellers showed he might be the answer, scoring 20 points. Sellers' play in the middle was complemented by forward Scott Burrell, whose 13 points, 8 rebounds, and 2 steals were critical in turning this East–West matchup around.

With UConn clinging to a 52–49 half-time lead, both teams were held scoreless for the first 2:28 of the second half, until Burrell ended the drought with a reverse underhand layup. Another minute had expired before someone scored again. This time Burrell saved the ball from going out of bounds and then dished off to Smith, who scored to extend the Huskies' lead to 56–49. That brought the Civic Center patrons to their feet, but the Soviets would quiet them with five unanswered points. The mini-run concluded with a Valeri Tikhonenko three-point goal. Tikhonenko was one of the few Soviets to solve the UConn press, finishing with a game-high 36 points.

Tikhonenko was one of just two on this particular squad who was in Seoul to bring home the gold to the Soviet Union. Tiik Sokk, the other gold-medal winner, was the Soviets' most potent weapon of this American visit. Against All-American Chris Jackson, Sokk scored 32 points. He added 23 against UNLV, the team that would eventually be champions of the NCAA. Against UConn Sokk scored just 10 points. Why? Chris Smith.

Smith's defense stymied the Soviets every time they pulled close to the Huskies. After a Calhoun time-out with 15:27 to play, and UConn up by just two, the Huskies broke out to a 63–56 lead when Steve Pikiell found Burrell streaking toward the basket. Burrell caught Pikiell's alley-oop pass and jammed it in, exhilarating the Civic Center crowd. Was this the beginning of the new UConn Huskies, or were the fans just being teased?

Sellers, after taking a feed from John Gwynn, would extend UConn's lead to nine, but Tikhonenko and the Soviets were not finished quite yet. Tikhonenko sank a three-point shot, and then Yuri Zhukanenko drove the length of the floor and scored to cut the lead to 67–62. Things became even more bleak when Sellers picked up his fifth foul attempting to block a Tikhonenko shot. Tikhonenko buried the two free throws and the Soviets were now within three. To make matters worse, Sellers' replacement, Dan Cyrulik, soon picked up his fifth foul. This forced Calhoun to move Toraino Walker into the pivot.

The answer to the Soviets' run came from an unlikely source. Murray Williams, ignoring the pain from a stress fracture in his knee that was limiting his playing time to two to three minute stretches, came off the bench and hit a jumper to make the score 69–64. His performance was reminiscent of the Williams who as a freshman keyed many a UConn run on the way to the NIT crown.

With 7:08 remaining in the game, Gwynn sank both ends of a one-and-one to give UConn its first double-digit lead, 79–69. The Huskies stretched it to a twelve-point lead before Tikhonenko again pulled the visitors close. UConn still had no answer for the high-flying Soviet, as he drew the foul from Walker. He converted the conventional three-point play and the Soviets were within striking distance at 83–76.

But UConn never allowed the Soviets to get closer than eight in the final four minutes of the game. The Huskies had pulled off the improbable; Calhoun's strategy had worked. Not only had UConn beaten the Soviets at the offensive and defensive ends, but on the boards as well. The Huskies outrebounded the Soviets 56–38. Against UNLV, the Soviets held the advantage over Larry Johnson and the rest of the Runnin' Rebels, 54–45. The win alone was bound to stir the hopes of Connecticut fans, and the post-game remarks were very encouraging.

Calhoun tried to keep the game in perspective by saying, "This is a young basketball team and it's going to have its up and downs," and, "We won't ever play a team like this again. We are not going to see people who pass up layups to get three-pointers." The Soviet National coach had other thoughts.

"The UConn team is just as good as the two other teams we've played . . . this team's defense is much better than the team of two games ago (UNLV)," Vladas Garastas said.

So, the obvious question to be asked was: If the Huskies were supposedly better defensively than the number one team in the nation, what could the fans expect from this youthful group of Huskies? Calhoun, who just wanted to put a competitive group on the floor, was left to consider the future. "The game itself was a pleasant surprise, but it was no shocker by any stretch of the imagination," he said. Calhoun said he fears losing, but adds that when the ball is tossed in the air he sees no reason why his team should lose. Against the Soviets, his team didn't see any reason to lose either.

Even after such a victory, questions remained. Who would start in UConn's season opener in two weeks? Was this game with the Soviets really that big a deal? Consider that Tikhonenko and Sokk were the only Soviets to have played on the Olympic squad that won the gold medal; the Soviets had to travel Sunday for the Monday game with UConn after a Saturday game at LSU; and Garastas said that only five of the Soviets on the floor that night would play in the World Championships in Argentina in the summer of 1990.

Despite the asterisks, Connecticut fans might have felt this was the year for change. Some probably thought in light of Garastas' comments the Huskies were ready right then to make a run at the NCAA tournament. Calhoun knew better at the time. "As far as the comments after the game, were we surprised? I can't say we knew we were going to be 31-6, or that we were going to win the Big East, but I did say that we were going to be better [than the 1988–89 team]."

Calhoun added, "I did say, though, that you were going to grow to like this team." Indeed, UConn, the Big East, and many other fans of NCAA basketball probably held a small place in their hearts for these lovable Huskies after the season was over. But back in November, most everyone beyond the Constitution State had not even heard of this group. Their work was just beginning, in more ways than one. No better place to start than on a 4,000-mile odyssey to the Great White North, Alaska.

Chapter 3

Alaska Shootout
November 24–26, 1989

After the defeat of the Soviet National team in Hartford, the expectations of Connecticut basketball fans were heightened. For a team that was supposed to be in a transitional phase, the Huskies were suddenly burdened by the reality that their fans were hungry for more immediate success. The pressure was certainly there, but fortunately for the Huskies they would have a chance to get away from those pressures, at least for their next three games. In the relative serenity of Anchorage, Alaska, UConn began its run.

Shadowed by the awesomeness that is the United States' highest point, Mt. McKinley, and overlooking the Gulf of Alaska Inlet, sits the city of Anchorage. Despite being nearly twice as populous as Hartford, Anchorage's sluggish economy in the winter months leaves its downtown streets mostly empty. Were it not for the Great Alaska Shootout there would have been even less activity. The streets were constantly covered with snow, and the daylight lasted just six hours a day.

It was Thanksgiving 1989. The players would not be spending the holiday with their families; instead, they would be nurturing their own family centered on the game of basketball. This process of team bonding was eased by Calhoun, who knew that leaving the players alone would help them get to know each other. "I was able to manipulate them and have them understand one another a lot better away from everything," he said.

Because of the Thanksgiving recess, there were no missed classes for the team to be concerned with—another factor that Calhoun attributed to a lessening of pressure on his team. That release of tensions showed up in the horsing around the players did in the hotel and when they ventured out into the city without a coach watching their every step. But there were times when the players and coaches did come together.

As a team, they witnessed wild Alaskan moose and met some of the native Eskimos. Then there was the ride on, what else, a Husky dogsled. Whether the season would have been as successful without the trip to the Great White North is debatable, but in the course of a season every moment that breeds teamwork is crucial.

One player who missed part of the fun was Nadav Henefeld. The twenty-one-year-old forward was granted permission by the NCAA to play one game for the Israeli national team on November 22. Henefeld caught a flight to Israel on November 18, practiced with the Israeli team, scored 23 points in a 99–93 victory over France, got on a plane two hours later, and arrived in Anchorage via New York and Seattle twenty-six hours later. There he joined his teammates, who were preparing for the first round of the tournament.

The pre-tournament banquet was the last opportunity for the participants to enjoy some camaraderie before the competition began. Texas A&M Coach Shelby Metcalf took off his coaching hat and put on his comical one. In his thick southern drawl, he explained the lack of respect his team got as it was overshadowed by the success of the Aggie football team. He also entertained with a couple of stories. Metcalf told of when he was in college and wanted to show his mother his new haircut. However, the only picture he had of himself at the time was one of him in the shower. Metcalf cut the picture in half in order to spare his mother the sight of the inappropriate part. The silver-haired Metcalf said he sent the wrong half, writing on the back of it, "How do you like my haircut?" He continued, "My mother wrote back and said, 'The haircut is nice, but you have to do something about that beard.'" The crowd laughed, and a few more tensions were relieved, at least until the games began.

Once the fun was over for the Huskies, the task of winning the twelfth annual season-opening tournament had begun. The importance of such a tournament was clear to UConn. First, it allowed the Huskies to play thirty regular-season games, because games in the non-contiguous states (Alaska, Hawaii) do not count toward a team's allotment of twenty-seven regular-season games. This might help the Huskies reach seventeen wins, typically the watermark for Big East teams making the NCAA tournament field of sixty-four.

Secondly, UConn would be playing nationally recognized teams early in the season. Even though the field did not have a pre-season Top Twenty team, the reputations of the teams at the Shootout were noteworthy. From the ranks of Division II came Alaska-Anchorage, the tournament host. UAA entered with a 10–23 Shootout record against the Division I powerhouses. UAA also had scored an upset win over eventual national champion Michigan the previous season.

The field also included Auburn, Florida State, Hawaii, and co-favorites Kansas State and Michigan State. But Texas A&M, under twenty-seventh-year head coach Shelby Metcalf, would be the first college team to meet the Huskies in the 1989–90 season. The Aggies had finished 1988–89 with a 16–14 record, and four of their top five scorers were back.

In the tournament opener, Michigan State upended Auburn 92–79. Connecticut versus Texas A&M would follow, then Kansas State would play Florida State and Hawaii would face UAA. The first-round winners would advance into the championship rounds Saturday and Monday, while the losers would face off against each other on Saturday and Sunday.

The importance of winning game one was not solely for championship purposes; the victors' remaining two games in the tournament would be seen nationwide on ESPN. Such exposure would help familiarize the rest of the nation with the Huskies. Unfortunately, UConn fell in the opener, 92–81.

After playing seemingly unbeatable basketball against the Soviets, the Huskies went as cold as the arctic air. Opening for UConn were Scott Burrell and Rod Sellers at the forward positions, Dan Cyrulik at center, and Chris Smith and Tate George in the backcourt.

The Huskies were challenged from the start: there were seven lead changes and three ties in the first thirteen minutes. However, A&M's Lynn Suber gradually took control of the game. In the first half, the 6'2" guard became a one-man Husky wrecking crew by scoring 26 points and hitting 6 of 6 from three-point range. Neither Smith, George, nor any other Husky could contain Suber. He teamed with Tony Milton to help spark a 14-4 run late in the half. Texas A&M led 51-37 at halftime, thanks to 54.8 percent field goal shooting.

Considering the way UConn prided itself on

defense, the first half was an embarrassment. In 1988–89 UConn allowed just over 60 points per game, and here the Aggies had nearly achieved that already. Calhoun said that after his team allowed Suber to shoot so freely in the first half it never recovered. The invincibility the Huskies thought they possessed was suddenly disappearing into the Alaskan dusk.

UConn's offensive performance was also less than impressive. Cyrulik (12 points) was the unlikely Husky leading scorer in the first half. But while Cyrulik was playing well on UConn's end, David Harris, a 6'10" junior college transfer, was playing well for A&M in the paint.

Harris finished the game with 11 rebounds, 3 blocked shots, and 9 points. His presence forced UConn to tighten up defensively, leaving Suber and Milton open from the outside.

With UConn down by fifteen, Cyrulik led the UConn charge. The seven-foot center hit an eight-foot hook shot, igniting a 9–3 run that pulled the Huskies within seven, 58–51. Then Texas A&M extended its lead to eleven, forcing UConn to take desperation three-point attempts.

In retrospect, UConn's first "official" game of the season was a shocker. "We were stunned, and we acted like a young team in that situation," Calhoun said. What the Huskies did learn was that they were indeed vulnerable. As a spanking is beneficial at times to a young child, so in the same respect is a blowout defeat good for a young team like the Huskies.

Cyrulik finished with a career-high 18 points and grabbed 9 rebounds in just twenty-one minutes of play. Cyrulik's point output was second only to Smith (19 points). While the sophomore from Bridgeport collected 4 assists and 2 steals, he also turned the ball over four times.

The rest of the Huskies fared little better. UConn, which would thrive on its opponents' mistakes in the future, turned the ball over fifteen times. The Huskies did show promise in the steal category; they collected nine, four by the well-traveled Henefeld. Henefeld only scored five, which may have been one reason he was not yet a household name in Connecticut. But his popularity and his number of steals would end up growing proportionately.

The individual statistics shed some light on why the Huskies lost this contest. Those who were expected to contribute more did not. Burrell and George both scored just 8 points while Sellers was held to 4 points. All of these numbers added up to UConn's first opening game loss in six seasons.

The Huskies might have been out of the running for the Shootout title, but there was still a lot to prove to themselves and their fans. Putting the loss behind them was critical. In retrospect, that is exactly what the Huskies did. And what about the Aggies? Metcalf would say the UConn game was his team's best effort all year. In fact, the Aggies would flounder to a 14–17 record and Metcalf would be fired midway through the season.

The Huskies still had two Shootout games to play. Their next opponent was Auburn, a first-round victim of eventual Shootout champion Michigan State. UConn started impressively in the first half, taking the play to the Tigers. The Huskies pressured Auburn into 18 first-half turnovers and just 30 percent shooting from the floor. They led, 48–27, at the break.

Henefeld's thievery continued, this time with 6 steals. The forward also scored 16 points, hitting 3 of 3 from three-point range. Scott Burrell rebounded from a disappointing game to turn in a big performance. He totaled 13 points, 9 rebounds, and 6 assists in twenty-six minutes. Not only did Burrell help balance UConn's running game, he also stripped the Tigers of the ball six times.

Chris Smith was another Husky playing both ends of the floor extremely well. The 6'2" guard had 17 points (8 of 8 on free throws), 5 assists, and 4 steals.

The Tigers came out strong in the second half and worked on chipping away at the huge UConn lead. In the second half Auburn shot 9 of 12 on three-pointers and 60.6 percent overall in the second half. The Tigers also forced 25 UConn turnovers in the game.

But this night belonged to the Huskies. They shot a blistering 6 of 7 from three-point range in the second half, and a school-record 10 of 18 for the game. Rod Sellers had 19 points and 9 rebounds, while John Gwynn added 14 points in the Huskies' 95–81 victory.

As the Texas A&M game was a learning experience for the Huskies, the Auburn contest was too. Calhoun was able to experiment with a number of combinations. Four of the five starters played at least twenty-one minutes. And UConn's bench outscored Auburn's 34-10.

Before leaving Alaska, the Huskies had one more game and a chance to get fourth place in the tournament. Their next opponent was Florida State, which had defeated Alaska-Anchorage in the losers' bracket. The Seminoles' headliner was point guard Tharon Mayes, from New Haven. "Ron-Ron," as he was called, would have to be contained if UConn was going to knock off the 1988–89 Metro Conference regular-season champion.

Back in 1986, Mayes was a hot prospect who considered attending UConn before winding up in Tallahassee. He had scored 50 points in FSU's first two tournament games, but the Huskies limited him to just 6 points in the first half as UConn built a 19-point lead, and led by 12 at the break. The Huskies stayed with their perimeter game, taking thirteen three-point shots in the first half, but connecting on only five. In the second half UConn went away from the outside game and tried to work the ball down low to Sellers and Cyrulik.

The crowd of 3,179 was the smallest audience the Huskies would play in front of during the season. The Alaskan fans wanted some excitement, this being a rare opportunity to see a prime time sporting event. UConn's defense would oblige, allowing the Seminoles to mount a 19-9 run. UConn was also into the penalty with nine minutes left in the game.

Florida State took advantage of the Huskies' charity and seized a 58-55 lead with less than five minutes to go. UConn cut the lead to one when Smith (team-high 14 points) found a fast-breaking Henefeld for the layup. Moments later Henefeld would come up big again, providing the most exciting moment of his brief collegiate career.

With the Huskies down one, Henefeld stole the ball from Mayes and scored to give UConn back the lead. Calhoun later credited Henefeld's big play to the 3-1-1 defense, which in time would receive plenty of praise nationwide. It was

Henefeld's third steal of the game, giving him thirteen for the season. Suddenly "Hene-who?" became Henefeld.

But it wasn't over yet. Sellers missed his third consecutive free throw and Seminole Aubry Boyd grabbed the rebound, dribbled downcourt, and buried a 10-foot jumper. With less than twenty seconds to play, Henefeld grabbed center stage again, calmly sinking his only two free throws of the game for a 61-60 lead. UConn's defense then held one last time, and Burrell hit a pair of insurance foul shots to wrap up the 63-60 victory.

"I think we played with character," Calhoun said following the game, "especially to have a good team make a run at us and for us to respond the way we did." The coach also was pleased to be coming home from the long trip 2-1. "That is good for a young team," he said.

The trip was indeed an educational experience. The Huskies learned more about each other during the week than they would have learned at home. They also lost an invincibility complex they might have had after the Soviet game. Then there were the two wins. "We beat two good 'name teams,'" Calhoun said. "They were good but probably not as good as their name. So psychologically we felt better." Chris Smith took home his first trophy of the season; he was named to the All-Tournament team as a result of his 60 points, 13 assists, and 6 steals. Calhoun got to see his new players in action away from the team's large media following, known as "The Horde." It consisted of writers from about twenty in-state publications, eight of whom traveled with the team to Alaska. The Huskies got a chance to be away from it all, sort of a retreat from the daily routine.

For the tournament, Michigan State won the title, Kansas State finished second, Hawaii third, and UConn fourth. Texas A&M, Florida State, Auburn, and UAA took the fifth through eighth spots, respectively. Even though many in Alaska were disappointed with the field, three of the teams (Kansas State, MSU, and UConn) would eventually receive bids to the NCAA tournament, and MSU and UConn would be regional top seeds.

The Huskies returned home a bit wiser about

each other and their game. How would a trip like this affect the rest of their season? Calhoun would eventually sum up the success of the road trip this way: "The basketball aspect, yes [we learned a lot], but in the social aspect [the players] really were able to understand one another."

Chapter 4

Lump-Sum Games I

November 30, December 2, 1989

Back on native soil, the Huskies prepared for Yale and what might have been called the beginning of the farewell tour for the UConn Field House. The Huskies would play just five more games in the thirty-five-year-old building before moving into the $28.1 million Harry A. Gampel Pavilion.

The Yale game was the fifty-sixth between the in-state rivals, and Calhoun was after his 300th coaching victory in eighteen seasons at Northeastern and UConn. Theoretically, the Huskies figured to have very little trouble. In 1988–89 they had blasted the Elis, 75–44, at Yale. Besides, what chance does an Ivy League school have against a team from the Big East? Well, if one's memory is short, Princeton came within one point of knocking Georgetown out of the 1989 NCAA tournament and scoring one of the all-time greatest upsets.

Like Princeton did to Georgetown, Yale would look to slow down the tempo against the Huskies. Calhoun was concerned about this and tried to formulate his defensive pressure accordingly.

The night before the game, Murray Williams underwent surgery on his injured left knee. The junior forward would miss the next seven games, and the Huskies could have used his offensive skills early in the Yale game.

UConn led, 33–21, at the half, but Yale dictated the tempo early and controlled it throughout the game. "We just had no rhythm, and their style of play tried to dictate that," Calhoun said. Added co-captain Tate George, "They [Yale] lull you to sleep with their play. Their picks get you frustrated, and they run the same thing at you."

The Huskies opened the second half with a 15–2 run. Such rallies would become a trademark of this club. Burrell started the flurry by banking in a jumper and sinking the ensuing free throw. Burrell would finish with 15 points and 8 rebounds, the third consecutive game he would score in double figures and grab at least 8 boards.

Gwynn followed a Yale miss with a three-pointer, and the UConn lead became twenty as Henefeld drove for a layup.

Yale tried to counter, but only got two free throws from Travis McCready. Then "Dove"

Nadav Henefeld (40) and Lyman DePriest (23) share good position for this rebound against Yale. UConn's control of the boards weighed heavily in their win over the Elis.

Henefeld drilled a three-pointer for 3 of his 13 second-half points (15 for the game).

Three-point shooting would be critical if the Huskies were to become a perimeter-oriented team. The eighteen attempts against Auburn emphasized that point. Against Yale, UConn launched fourteen three-point attempts, hitting six. Long-range shooters Gwynn and Smith both hit two, while forwards Burrell and Henefeld each added one more.

Calhoun, whose record was now 300–184, downplayed the milestone. "It just means that I have been coaching a long time," he said. The coach was more concerned about the game itself.

Rod Sellers calls for the ball down low, where he used his height advantage for 8 points, 4 rebounds, and 2 blocked shots.

"We should have overmatched them with our size. I'm not totally pleased. We have to get better," he said. A twenty-six-point victory was nice, but Calhoun was trying to convince his players they were very beatable, even against a team such as Yale.

The first of UConn's "lump-sum" games was over. They were contests in which Calhoun believed the Huskies should have little trouble. "In years past, before we got here, Connecticut had the tremendous history of taking those games

and making them three-point games," he said. "That doesn't instill the kind of confidence you are going to need later on against some of the great teams."

Two days after the Yale victory, UConn faced Howard University for the first time ever. What made UConn so unpredictable in 1989–90 was who would take charge of the team in a given game. Against Howard it would be Tate George.

Sellers shoots over Yale's Stuart Davies.

Chris Smith (shooting) pulls up for a jumper off a Dan Cyrulik (55) screen. Smith scored 11 points as part of UConn's balanced offensive attack against Howard University.

In seasons past George had been mocked by some of the fans, and had been the recipient of many a Calhoun tongue-lashing. But he looked to put things behind him his senior year. The added responsibility of being a co-captain helped turn George's work ethic around. After Calhoun told him that he might not start during the 1989–90 season, George worked incessantly on his game. Before the Howard game, though, George had just 29 points in four games, and had yet to score in double digits.

It was George's three-point goal that put UConn ahead, 13–5, early in the game and

electrified the Field House crowd. Howard cut the lead to 15–10 before UConn took control of the game. The Huskies allowed Howard just five points in the next ten minutes, and took a 42–24 lead into the locker room. George scored 11 of his 15 points in the half, while sixth-man Gwynn added 7.

In the second half UConn quickly extended its lead to twenty-three on a Chris Smith three-pointer. Smith would finish with 11 points, once again proving Calhoun's theory that the offensive structure of the team was not centered around any one player. "You can take the system and simply say that it could greatly benefit any individual player on the team. That made it so much easier psychologically for the kids to share the wealth," said Calhoun, who holds a degree in sociology.

In contrast to the first four games, George and Smith's roles appeared to have reversed. Smith was the one dishing off (9 assists against Howard), many times to George. Dan Cyrulik improved his status by grabbing 15 rebounds, a career high. Sellers (11 points) took over the scoring down low. UConn outscored the Bison 44–16 in the paint, and outrebounded them 54–32. The Huskies converted 21 offensive rebounds into 22 second-chance points.

As the game got out of hand, Calhoun gave many of his substitutes important playing time. Toraino Walker played thirteen minutes, Lyman DePriest eleven, and Nadav Henefeld sixteen. Steve Pikiell played six minutes, and his brother Tim, Marc Suhr, and Oliver Macklin also saw action. The last three players gradually were learning their roles for UConn.

With 8:30 to play, UConn built its biggest lead at 64–31. A minute later, Burrell added his own exclamation point by jamming home Smith's alley-oop pass.

The 78–59 win gave UConn a 4–1 record and made Calhoun a happy coach. He was especially pleased with his team's intensity and ball move-

Tate George releases an eight-footer surrounded by opponents . . .

. . . and hits the mark for two of his team-high 15 points against Howard.

31

Huskies would end up, games like this added weeks to the players' maturation into Calhoun's system.

"In both those games, the system worked. And it became more and more ingrained in the kids that the system would work," Calhoun said. "These two games were important because we came, we saw, and we got them."

Sellers turned in another solid performance at the forward position, scoring 11 points for the Huskies. Here he goes up for a strong move over Charles Chase.

Cyrulik and George trap Bison Keith Kirvin in the corner. The Howard forward was held to just 2 points in the Husky victory.

ment. Calhoun always stressed finding the open man, and his team was seeing the benefits.

"We seemed to have the tremendous ability to go out against a team that we were superior to and just strangle them," Calhoun said after the season. This was just one aspect where UConn of 1989–90 would try to separate itself from the UConn teams of the past. Considering where the

Chapter 5

Just Another Challenge
December 4, 1989

The problem with early-season games for many of the top-rated teams in the nation is the lack of competition. For instance, Georgetown's first three games of the season were against Hawaii-Loa, Hawaii-Pacific, and Florida International. It was not just the Hoyas, though; many teams in big conferences load up on patsies. So, in order to give the players challenging games early in the season, Big East commissioner Dave Gavitt and Atlantic Coast Conference boss Gene Corrigan came up with the ACC–Big East Challenge.

The purpose, in theory, was to prove which conference was stronger. The eight teams in the ACC and the nine in the Big East would be ranked. The pre-season number ones would square off, and so on all the way down to number eight (the ninth team in the Big East would sit out). Each conference would earn a point for each victory, and the conference with the most points at the end of the challenge is declared the winner. According to pre-season selections, UConn figured to finish eighth in the Big East. That meant a matchup with the Mary-land Terrapins on Monday, December 4.

Maryland had finished the previous season with a disappointing 1–13 record in the ACC, and the forecast for 1989–90 was no better. The Terrapins did have three starters back, including 6'10" forward Jerrod Mustaf. The sophomore had averaged 14.3 points and 7.8 rebounds in 1988–89. And there was 6'9" Tony Massenburg (16.6 p.p.g., 7.8 r.p.g.).

Tate George said prior to the Challenge he didn't want the Huskies to be the only Big East team to lose. Whether he was extremely confident in the conference's chances, or he was just kidding was not clear. After the first night of the Challenge, it was obvious George's words were not very prophetic.

The first night of action would be at the Hartford Civic Center. The opener featured number three seeds, Pittsburgh and Georgia Tech, followed by Connecticut versus Maryland.

As if Connecticut's media horde was not enough, national publications such as *Sports Illustrated* and media from the three other schools were all there—making the Challenge's

Nadav Henefeld shoots from the outside over the outstretched hand of Maryland's Walt Williams (42). The Huskies opened up the floor against the taller Terrapins with good outside shooting and a full court game plan.

first night look more like an NCAA tournament game than a couple of regular-season matchups.

All of the games of the Challenge were televised on ESPN, giving schools such as UConn some rare national television exposure. Of course, Georgia Tech and Pittsburgh made it very difficult for UConn and Maryland, or anyone else for that matter, to upstage this inaugural game.

With the game clock about to expire, Georgia Tech's Dennis Scott nailed a fall-away one-handed shot to give the Yellow Jackets a thrilling 93–92 comeback victory. It became clear the Challenge's point was not to prove which conference was best, but to provide exciting basketball for the fans. Besides, what difference did it really make which conference was better? Chris Smith answered that by saying, "I wanted to prove that the Big East was better."

Going beyond the debate of what purpose a meeting like this means for either conference, there was another game to play. The Huskies, who wore their visiting blue uniforms because the Civic Center was considered a neutral court for this game, started the same five players they had so far this year: Rod Sellers and Scott Burrell at the forward positions, Tate George and

Chris Smith in the backcourt, and Dan Cyrulik in the middle. Except for the 7′ Cyrulik, the Terrapins held a clear height advantage over the Huskies. Calhoun's game plan was obvious: prevent the game from being played in the paint by pressing and running the entire length of the court.

Rod Sellers slips inside for a layup during UConn's win over the Terrapins.

Calhoun recalled, "When the game starts out and they line up against us, there were some snickers, 'These little guys from Connecticut are going to get killed.'" UConn did not seem to care about height advantages or disadvantages, as long as it implemented the defensive system that had worked so well thus far. Not only would the Huskies do that, but they would also see the offensive return of Chris Smith.

The Huskies led, 8–6, when Smith stepped forward and sparked an 11–0 run. He scored 7 of UConn's first 14 points on his way to a 15-point first half. That was not the only problem the

Terrapins had to face. With just under five minutes gone in the first half, Maryland guard Teyon McCoy pushed off as he drove the baseline. The foul was his third, forcing Maryland coach Gary Williams to sit him down.

The Huskies continued to cruise, not letting the Terrapins get their inside game on track. In fact, it was the quartet of Burrell, Sellers, Cyrulik, and Henefeld that helped UConn outscore Maryland 32–18 in the paint for the game. The four also combined for 26 rebounds as UConn outrebounded the Terrapins 45–38.

UConn led, 49–33, at the half, and there was

John Gwynn makes a move on Williams—Maryland's 6'8" guard.

not much of a challenge left. The Huskies maintained the large lead in the second half with the continual help of their defense. They forced 27 Maryland turnovers and had 18 steals leading to 31 points. With Calhoun's system in full gear, the defense gave the offense critical scoring opportunities.

The UConn defense tightened up even more in the second half, allowing Maryland to hit just 11 of 30 from the floor. Miscues by UConn were the only thing preventing them from winning by an even larger margin. For the game, UConn would turn the ball over seventeen times, many of those in the second half. Connecticut still had the game in hand, though, and easily wound up winning 87–65.

Once the game appeared secure, Connecticut fans turned their attention to Tate George, who

Coach Jim Calhoun gives instructions to his players on the bench.

Gwynn made good use of his twenty-one minutes by scoring 11 points (4 for 9) and tying George and Smith for the team lead with 5 assists. Here he dishes out to Lyman DePriest (23) on the wing.

was closing in on Karl Hobbs' all-time UConn assist mark of 534. George finished with 5 assists, leaving him just shy and forcing Connecticut fans to wait until UConn faced Hartford three nights later.

Smith finished the game with 22 points and 5 assists. Henefeld and Burrell both scored 11 while Gwynn and Sellers each added 10.

"It never became a game that was played 10–12 feet around the basket," Calhoun said. "It became a 94-foot game where our quickness and our skills both defensively and offensively took over."

A national television audience had gotten its first look at these Huskies, and it certainly would not be the last. Connecticut's impressive victory was the only blowout in the inaugural ACC–Big East Challenge, which ended in a 4–4 tie. Did this mean Connecticut was better than the conference's number eight team? Even with the answers Calhoun was getting six games into the season, more questions arose. How would the Huskies fare against the likes of Georgetown, Syracuse, Villanova, and the rest of Big East field? The answers would have to wait about a week, until after UConn played two more "lump-sum" games.

Chapter 6

Lump-Sum Games II
December 7, 9, 1989

In the second installment of UConn's "lump-sum" games, the team looked to re-emphasize its potent press and the system that had become its main weapon. The games against the University of Hartford Hawks and the Maine Black Bears again figured to be relatively easy Big East warm-ups.

The Hawks, of the North Atlantic Conference, share the same part-time home court with Connecticut—the Hartford Civic Center. That might have been the only notable factor of the contest. Calhoun, though, did not take this team lightly. He still remembered 1986-87, his inaugural season at UConn, when the Huskies lost to Hartford, 49-48, on their way to a 9-19 campaign.

A near-capacity crowd (13,102) at the Civic Center watched the action between two schools that were a mere half-hour apart. But the absence of any longtime tradition between the two prevented any hype concerning statewide supremacy.

Calhoun approached the game as another chance to ingrain his system in his players' minds. Specific players began to emerge as the key scorers and rebounders, while others contributed in less glamorous roles.

Chris Smith led all Husky scorers with 16 points. The other starters also filled their roles: Cyrulik grabbed 9 rebounds, Burrell 7, and Rod Sellers 6. Tate George chipped in 12 points and 6 assists.

This game marked a special occasion for George and the Connecticut faithful who had watched him grow through his four years in Storrs. With 9:56 gone in the first half, George fed Gwynn on the right side of the court and Gwynn hit a three-pointer. This gave George 535 career assists, and the school record. The crowd acknowledged the play of the club's lone senior with a resounding ovation.

Calhoun's fear of a lackluster performance against an inferior team never came to pass, though the game was far from a clinic. In the first half, the Hawks booted, bobbled and blundered the ball away 17 times (28 overall), while the Huskies made 12 turnovers (21 total). Ball-handling aside, the Huskies gained a 39-21 lead at the half en route to a 79-54 victory.

Against Maine the story was somewhat different. True the outcome was the same (a blow-out win by the Huskies), but the sloppy play of the opposition did not rub off on UConn this game. A 95–55 win over a Northeast Conference foe may not seem too impressive, but it was the execution of Calhoun's system that set the tone for the Husky-style thrashing.

Connecticut scored 26 points off 24 Maine turnovers and netted 22 points on fast breaks. In turn, the Huskies turned the ball over just 11 times. Sellers began to show his ability in the paint, hitting 11 of 12 shots for a career-high 22

Guard Chris Smith jams home a dunk. He led all Husky scorers with 16 points in their win over the Hartford Hawks.

points. Henefeld came off the bench to grab 11 boards and make 4 steals. By halftime the Huskies had doubled up on Maine, 44–22, as the Black Bears could manage just two field goals in the last twelve minutes of the half.

UConn center Dan Cyrulik (55) battles Hartford's David Thompson (11) for a rebound under the net. Cyrulik collected 9 rebounds to lead the Huskies.

Smith also hit several shots from the outside including 1 for 3 from three-point land.

Even freshmen Tim Pikiell and Oliver Macklin saw playing time for the Huskies in the second half. Tate George scored 10 points to go with 8 assists.

The win gave Calhoun his longest winning streak since coming to Connecticut and helped set up the team for the season's main event—the Big East schedule. The Huskies, now 7–1, used these games to their advantage. They helped Calhoun accentuate the importance of his sys-

Perhaps Larry Griffiths (13) would have been better off passing than trying to shoot over Tate George. George gets "all ball" on this shot attempt.

Griffiths tries to return the favor on this double pump reverse layup by George, who scored 12 points.

tem that would aid the team in coming months. With matchups against teams like Georgetown, Syracuse, and St. John's on the way, UConn would need to know Calhoun's system, and more importantly how to execute it. However, it would take time for the Huskies to parlay the experience into success in the Big East. A case in point was the conference opener against Villanova.

More importantly, in the Hartford game George set the new University of Connecticut record for career assists, breaking Karl Hobbs' mark of 534 assists.

Scott Burrell concentrates on his layup as a Hawk defender streaks past him.

Chapter 7

No Respect
December 12, 1989

At the Big East pre-season press conference in New York's Grand Hyatt Hotel, the media swarmed around coaches John Thompson of Georgetown and Jim Boeheim of Syracuse. No surprise there; the Hoyas and Orangemen were picked in a virtual dead heat to finish atop the conference. Georgetown would get the nod, though, as the favorite. The Hoyas were the defending conference regular-season and post-season champions. Thompson's Hoyas also had the luxury of returning the twin towers of 6'10" Alonzo Mourning and 7'2" Dikembe Mutombo. Despite losing Charles Smith to the NBA, the Georgetown guards looked just as strong in 1989–90, with the return of seniors Mark Tillmon and Dwayne Bryant.

Syracuse also returned a mother lode of talent. Senior guard Stephen Thompson had averaged 18.0 points a game in 1988–89, and power forward Derrick Coleman averaged 16.9 points. Complementing the play of this duo was 6'9" sophomore Billy Owens (13.0 p.p.g.). Losing guards Sherman Douglas (18.2 p.p.g.) and Matt Roe (11.0 p.p.g.) seemed to be the only dark spot

in Boeheim's bid for his second NCAA Final Four appearance. During the press conference, Boeheim expressed that it would be a disappointment if his team did not make it to Denver for the 1990 Final Four.

Big East Commissioner Dave Gavitt watched the affair from the platform in the front of the room. Gavitt had coached Providence, the U.S. Olympic team in the boycott year of 1980 and was the father of the Big East Conference. Entering its eleventh season, the conference was considered to be one of the best, if not the best, in the nation. Six of its nine teams had made the Final Four, two had won national championships, and all but one, UConn, had been to the NCAA tournament since 1979.

In 1989–90 the Big East would experiment with the new six-foul rule. In all conference games, players would be allowed to collect six fouls before being forced to leave the game. This was intended to leave the league's stars around a little longer each game, thus satisfying the fans. Six of the nine coaches were in favor; Paul Evans of Pittsburgh, Jim O'Brien of Boston College, and Jim Calhoun of Connecticut disapproved.

While the media members continued to swarm around the coaches from Syracuse and Georgetown and Commissioner Gavitt, getting their opinions on the new rule, a number of other reporters approached the other seven tables in the room. Some spoke with St. John's Lou Carnesecca, whose Redmen's success in 1989–90 would depend on the health of senior forward Jayson Williams, as well as guard Greg "Boo"

Harvey. St. John's, which finished an uncharacteristic seventh in the conference in 1988–89, was selected fourth for the upcoming season.

Pittsburgh's Panthers were tabbed for third, but an injury to floor leader Sean Miller made it a precarious pick. The fifth team, Providence, was looking for a little respect under second-year coach Rick Barnes. Eric Murdock (16.2 p.p.g.) and 6'10" center Marty Conlon (14.3 p.p.g.) were the Friars' leaders.

Dan Cyrulik (55) gets no respect from Villanova's Greg Woodard. Woodard also did major damage to the Huskies with his shooting, scoring 17 points.

Tom Greis (33) also gave UConn shooters a tough time of it on the inside with 3 blocked shots.

Chris Smith converts on a layup, but he scored only 12 points in a rare off-game.

Rollie Massimino's Villanova Wildcats were picked sixth, just behind Providence. Tom Greis, the 7'3" senior center, would lead the Wildcats. Two tables to the left of Massimino, between Carnesecca and Boeheim, sat P. J. Carlesimo. Carlesimo and his Seton Hall Pirates shocked the college basketball world in 1989 by advancing all the way to the NCAA title game. Unfortunately for Carlesimo, all his starters from that team were gone.

Seated next to the doorway, Jim O'Brien was trying to explain how his Boston College team would compete. The Eagles were picked to finish ninth and had no double-digit scorers returning.

Right next to O'Brien, and tucked away in the left corner of the room, was Jim Calhoun. At the start of the press conference, three or four members of the media approached Calhoun. They asked him questions that implied his team did not have much of a chance to compete in the conference. Calhoun reiterated that his team was going to be fun to watch. Reality was in Calhoun's mind, though. How would his young group, playing against teams blessed with more height, speed, quickness, and depth, be able to compete, let alone win games? Tate George and Steve Pikiell also fielded questions, trying to sound optimistic.

Villanova and UConn would open the 1989–90 Big East season in the Hartford Civic Center in front of a near-capacity crowd of 14,947. The Huskies came in with a seven-game winning streak and a record of 7–1. The 4–3 Wildcats knew playing in Hartford was no easy task. In 1988 they lost to UConn 57–55 at the Civic Center.

The Hartford fans, as much as anyone, wanted the Huskies to dispel their pre-season conference ranking of eighth. Unfortunately, at the time UConn did not have the ability to do so. The press

Lyman DePriest makes a nifty move on a reverse layup—one way to avoid the reach of Greis (33).

The UConn Husky mascot shows off a few moves of his own during a break.

Scott Burrell was a bright spot in UConn's 1989–90 Big East opener, scoring 18 points in a starting role against Villanova.

that heretofore had worked so effectively did not appear early in the first half as the Wildcats had their way. Gradually UConn began to force Villanova turnovers, but the hosts shot a season-low 20.6 percent in the half and trailed 31–16 at the break. The fans voiced their displeasure.

The boos were heard nationwide on ESPN, and commentator Dick Vitale even blasted the jeering fans. It was not a good start to the Big East season for UConn, though the Huskies did improve during the second half. Their defense held the Wildcats to just 19 shots in the second half, while providing the offense some scoring opportunities.

The Huskies managed to outscore Villanova 41–33 in the second half, but the winning streak was over. The 64–57 loss, like the defeat to Texas A&M, proved the Huskies were still a vulnerable team. Perhaps a change in the attitude of the players, or a change in the lineup, would help shake things up.

The Huskies would have thirteen days off before their next game, giving them time to study for exams and concentrate on the remainder of the season. With the excellent play of the defense thus far, things were not as bleak as they might have appeared. The increased number of scoring opportunities they were getting from the defense might be just enough to overcome the sub-par shooting. It was not good enough against Villanova, though, leaving some to wonder that maybe the pre-season critics were correct.

Cyrulik releases a short jump-hook in the paint.

Time winds down on the Huskies as Tate George goes up for a shot. The two teams traded baskets, but the Wildcats eventually won by the same 7-point margin.

Chapter 8

Happy Husky Holidays
December 23, 29, 30, 1989

During the holidays, as the Christmas carol goes, your sweetheart gives to you, among other things, three French hens, two turtle doves, and a partridge in a pear tree. After the performance against Villanova, Jim Calhoun would be satisfied with just three wins.

No one knew quite why UConn scheduled a game against Southern Connecticut State, a Division II school. Calhoun figured his team should win by at least 20 points. He was only off by 43. The 100–37 romp was UConn's largest margin of victory since 1919–20.

Every Husky who showed up for the game played. Calhoun was confident enough before the game that he let Lyman DePriest head back early to Highland Park, Michigan, for Christmas.

Chris Smith led the hosts with 20 points in only twenty-two minutes on the floor. Tate George added 12 and John Gwynn came off the bench to score 16. The Huskies set records for most three-point shots attempted (30) and made (11).

The Husky reserves used this game to their advantage. Toraino Walker banged the boards for a game-high 10 rebounds in fifteen minutes of action. Calhoun had brought the freshman from Orlando to UConn to eventually fill the void in the middle. Walker, using his upper-body strength, outmuscled the smaller Central Connecticut players underneath the basket and obtained good rebounding position.

Marc Suhr, the 7-footer from West Germany, scored 4 points and grabbed 5 rebounds in his nine minutes. Steve Pikiell, whose shoulder injury had kept him sidelined the year before, saw fifteen minutes of floor time. Calhoun continually praised the co-captain for his courage in coming back from the injury.

The Huskies' next two games were in the Connecticut Mutual Classic. The Classic was born in 1978 and has since been sponsored by the Connecticut Mutual Life Insurance Company and the university. Before that, from 1974–77, the "UConn Classic" was held for two years at the Field House and then moved to the Hartford Civic Center.

This year's guests were Mississippi State of the Southeastern Conference, St. Joseph's (Pa.) of the Atlantic 10, and Delaware of the East Coast Conference. UConn was out to repeat as tournament champion; the Huskies had won the Classic in 1988 by downing Harvard, 84–43, and Air Force, 68–55.

If Calhoun's Huskies can be considered a young team, than St. Joe's should be considered a group of infants, by comparison. Sophomore Chris Amos was back for coach Jim Boyle, and with him his 11.2 points per game. He would start at one guard position. Marlon Miller would be the big man in the paint for the Hawks as he too was back with his 6'7" frame and 8.1 points per game from last year.

For the opener against St. Joseph's, Calhoun would start Nadav Henefeld for the first time. Burrell and Sellers joined Henefeld up front while Smith and George formed the backcourt. They staked UConn to a 43–26 halftime lead, thus giving the reserves more time to strut their stuff.

Smith led all scorers for the game with 19 points. George added 14 and Gwynn, in his familiar off-the-bench role, scored 10 points. Henefeld continued his criminal ways, making five steals. UConn held the Hawks to just 30.2 percent field-goal shooting, including a combined 8 of 27 for the duo of Amos and Miller, in the 83–58 blow-out.

UConn's title game opponent was Mississippi State, who slipped by Delaware, 66–65, in the first game. Once again Henefeld was in the starting lineup for the 9–2 Huskies.

But it wasn't long before Calhoun could use his reserves for an extended period of time. Cyrulik, Gwynn, and Williams totaled forty-seven minutes on the court. Gwynn was again impressive in relief, averaging a point per minute with 14 points in fourteen minutes.

The Huskies were able to pull away in the first half by shooting nearly 56 percent from the field. They went into the locker room with a 46–29 lead. The Bulldogs came storming back in the second half. A 20-point Husky lead was cut to 11, before Henefeld countered with back-to-back hoops. The tournament MVP finished with a team-high 17 points and 6 steals. The Huskies shot a season-best 54.7 percent from the floor as they prevailed 84–68.

Calhoun was pleased that after two seemingly easier contests, the team was able to step up its play a notch. This was the season to be jolly, and now the Huskies were a happy 10–2 overall heading into the new year. Henefeld was beginning to show this part of the world what those in the Middle East already knew—that he was a big-time player. Now the Huskies' task was to take their confidence into the next stretch of the season, beginning with a return to Big East action in New York.

Chapter 9

New York Nightmare
January 2, 1990

The Huskies boarded their bus the day after the New Year's celebrations for the 130-mile trek to Jamaica, New York. For the St. John's Redmen, it was their first game of the Big East season, while the Huskies looked to rebound from a somewhat disappointing start in the conference race.

It would not be easy; since the Big East's birth in 1979, the Huskies had not won a game in St. John's Alumni Hall. And in the teams' twenty-two meetings, UConn had won merely three.

After beating their last three opponents by a combined score of 267–163, the Huskies believed they had turned the corner following the loss to Villanova. But Burrell and Henefeld would have to contain the Redmen's go-to guy, 6'10" Jayson Williams, and point guard Greg "Boo" Harvey.

Connecticut's guard tandem of Smith and George had continued to develop in the later games in December. Since the loss to Villanova, Smith had averaged 17.6 points and 5.3 assists. George's role was growing simultaneously; he had scored in double figures in six of the last eight games. The co-captain was becoming a leader on the court, too.

Despite the Huskies' strong play in their three previous games, St. John's was a different story. Williams, Harvey, and Malik Sealy keyed the Redmen's 68.9 percent field-goal shooting in the first half. St. John's walked off the court with a 48–32 halftime lead. The Huskies were once again getting a rude Big East awakening, as the ghosts of seasons past continued to haunt them.

UConn did have its chances. In the first half, with the help of its pressure defense, the visitors took 41 shots. But they hit just 14 of them. To make matters worse, the Huskies began launching three-point shots to try to cut into the deficit. This was to no avail, though, as they hit on only 1 of 10.

The Redmen defense was equally tough in the second half. Sealy, a 6'8" sophomore, had 5 of St. John's 13 steals in the game. For Connecticut, Henefeld had 5 steals and Smith 4, as UConn finished the game with 12 steals. It was the first time in the season that the opposition had more steals than the Huskies.

Stealing a basketball is somewhat of an art form. A player must have a keen eye to watch the ball, and he must have the peripheral vision necessary to watch the passing lanes. He must also be able to anticipate who will likely get the ball. Perhaps most important, he must have quick feet and, of course, hands. For the Huskies, no one did it better than Henefeld.

"The Dove" had played plenty of international basketball, where quickness has become an integral part of the game. He came to the U.S. looking for a university willing to take a chance on a player with an unusual, relatively unheard of, style of play. Henefeld went to St. John's on a recruiting trip and indeed might have ended up a New Yorker were it not for the lack of a traditional campus. St. John's (enrollment 19,500) has no dormitories, and its big-city atmosphere may not have been what Henefeld expected in an American university.

Then Calhoun invited Henefeld to visit UConn. The campus is twenty-seven miles from Hartford, surrounded by farmlands and situated in the usually quiet town of Storrs. And it has dormitories. Henefeld was sold. Against St. John's, Henefeld would score just 2 points, but his 5 steals and 5 rebounds exemplified his multi-faceted game.

No particular Husky stood out on this night. The Redmen outshot the Huskies from the field (68.6 percent to 32.5 percent), from three-point land (57.1 percent to 12.5 percent), and from the free throw line (65.5 percent to 50.0 percent). The end result was a 93–62 loss and an 0–2 record in the Big East. A little too early to write off the Huskies, but at this point they appeared doomed to the role of spoiler, or at best a team that would have to scratch its way into the NCAA tournament.

The road only got rockier. On tap were games against Pitt in Hartford, and on the road at Villanova and Seton Hall. Then came meetings with Syracuse and Georgetown in Hartford. Following the St. John's loss the Huskies were 10–3. If seventeen wins was the watermark for an NCAA bid for a Big East team, UConn would need to go 7–7 for the remainder of their conference schedule. The positives: the UConn defense was causing havoc through turnovers and steals, and some individuals were stepping forward on a team not dominated by one player. The negative points: the Huskies were prone to miserable shooting games, they were not always able to convert turnovers and steals into points, and their youth appeared to drag them down when they fell behind. Calhoun felt that the talent was there; it just had to be harnessed.

Chapter 10

The Swing Games
January 6–13, 1990

UConn's inability to tackle Big East foes in the same fashion as the lesser non-conference opponents seemed hauntingly familiar at this point in the schedule. Calhoun's view of his team's record was different than others. "There were a lot of misconceptions that we were down and out," he remembered, "but we were 10-3, and that's not down and out." But Connecticut was 0-2 in conference play, and that made the efforts over the next week more critical.

There were other troubling signs. Scott Burrell, who had started every game so far, would be sidelined for five games after having arthroscopic surgery on his knee. Then there was the upcoming schedule. UConn sports information director Tim Tolokan remembers the fear in the air during the period between the St. John's loss and the game against Pitt. "When you're 0-2 and you lose by 31—and I don't care if you're Jim Calhoun or [assistant coach] Howie Dickenman—you're in that damn locker room after the St. John's game, and you don't think you're ever going to win another game."

Pitt came into the contest off a loss to Syra-cuse. But the Panthers did have some offensive firepower. The Panthers returned three players who had averaged in double figures last year: Brian Shorter (19.6 p.p.g.), Jason Matthews (16.3 p.p.g.), and Bobby Martin (12.2 p.p.g.). Fortunately for the Huskies, they would not have to worry about dangerous point guard Sean Miller, who was out for the year with injuries.

With Burrell out, Calhoun moved Sellers to a forward position and reinserted Cyrulik at the center spot. This lineup gave the Huskies a little more bulk under the basket.

The first half saw the Huskies shoot almost 10 percent less from the field than the Panthers, but also take more than twice as many shots and thus go into the locker room up by six, 30–24. The defense and the system were working for Connecticut. In the second half, Pitt hit just 9 of 27 shots, while UConn went 13 for 25.

Shorter (14 points) and Martin (15 points) were contained by the UConn press, which helped force 26 turnovers. Meanwhile, the guard trio of Smith, George, and Gwynn accounted for 54 of the Huskies' 79 points.

"We were doing things well," Calhoun recounted after the 79–61 victory, "and I knew four to five minutes into the game that unless something drastic happened, we would win because the press showed that it was going to be a factor. You could see it coming, it was just a matter of time."

Next came the troublesome task of facing Villanova at the duPont Pavilion, where the Huskies had never won. Calhoun decided to move Murray Williams into the lineup at forward and shift Sellers to center. Cyrulik had been held scoreless in eighteen minutes of action against Pitt.

Everything went according to plan for the Huskies. They held the Wildcats to six field goals in the first half and eventually cruised to a 71–54 victory. Henefeld, Smith, and Sellers combined for 56 points. But it was a team effort on defense, with everyone contributing to the suffocating defensive pressure that resulted in 17 steals. In the Calhoun system, each player must remember his duties, and be in top physical condition, for it to work. Due to the fast-paced nature of the game, players will become fatigued during the forty minutes. Therefore, a bench with the ability to fill in at specific junctures is necessary for success. Calhoun had this in the Huskies.

Lyman DePriest was the Huskies' super-sub against Villanova. While he scored only 4 points in nineteen minutes, he pulled down 4 rebounds and was instrumental in the success of the press. But this game was really a showcase for Henefeld. In thirty-five minutes he amassed 19 points, 8 rebounds, and 6 steals.

Gil Santos, an announcer for the Big East Television Network, likened the Huskies' style to that of the Boston Celtics. "What it definitely comes down to is the fact that winning games comes from the neck up. The teams who take stupid shots, who don't make the extra pass, or who don't dedicate themselves to defense are going to lose," he said. "The [Celtic] teams I covered during the eighties won three world championships, and UConn played the same kind of way. That's how they were able to beat teams that were better athletically—they beat those teams by being smarter."

The smart, unselfish, dedicated-to-defense Connecticut squad had its first taste of what it felt like to foil the experts. The Huskies were now 2–2 in the Big East and had erased their own doubts. What would stop them from taking their success one step further? Nothing, as far as they were concerned.

The Huskies' road show moved north to the Meadowlands for their third game in seven days. Host Seton Hall didn't have any regulars back from their national runner-up team, but Frantz Volcy, Michael Cooper, and Anthony Avent all had been major contributors in 1988–89. Freshmen Terry Dehere and Daryl Crist comprised P. J. Carlesimo's backcourt.

The rookies were little match for the Huskies, who forced 23 turnovers (UConn made just 14). Henefeld played nearly the whole game (thirty-eight minutes) and recorded 6 steals and 14 points. Chris Smith and Tate George combined for 7 steals, as UConn finished with 18 steals compared to Seton Hall's 3.

UConn led, 42–31, at halftime and began to pull away in the second half. However, the Pirates put together a 10–0 run, and with just thirty-nine seconds left in the game, Seton Hall had cut the lead to 75–74. It was as close as the Pirates would get. Sellers, leaking out after a missed Pirates' shot, converted a Henefeld outlet pass into 2 of his team-high 19 points. The monstrous dunk ended the Huskies' scoring, and seconds later the final horn sounded on a 79–76 UConn victory.

This time it was John Gwynn who gave the Huskies instant energy off the bench. The team's sixth man scored 14 points in twenty-one minutes on the floor, including 2 of 3 from three-point territory.

The Huskies had just won three conference games in succession for the first time since 1982–83. They took from these games proof of their own unselfish system and a new level of confidence. The beauty of Calhoun's system was brought to light during these "swing games." The freedom to rotate a starting five according to who was hot along with a bench that could fill in at any time was a luxury Calhoun relished.

"If I had to think of the season, I would think of those three games in a row," said the coach.

"Pitt became critical, the other two became exclamation points. In the sense that we beat Villanova and Seton Hall on the road, I knew we had turned the corner. We were starting to roll and the rest of the stuff really started to fall into place.

"People would ask, and I would tell them that there were certain things that made it happen for us. I tell them that it was not Georgetown, Syracuse, and St. John's; it was Pitt, at Villanova, and at Seton Hall. When we came back and were 13-3, I knew we were going to be in the NCAA tournament. It was just a matter of how good we were going to be."

Chapter 11

The January Men
January 15, 20, 1990

Calhoun's Huskies returned home from their two-game road trip with a 3–2 record in the Big East. The confidence level was building on the team as well as with the fans. Both would face stiff tests of their faith. On Monday, January 15, on ESPN, the Huskies would host Syracuse at the Civic Center. Just five days later, John Thompson's Georgetown Hoyas would come in to Hartford.

Syracuse had spent six straight weeks on top of the Associated Press poll in the early part of the season. Only after a loss to Villanova in the Carrier Dome did the Orangemen fall from that spot. But they had rebounded with wins over St. John's and Boston College.

Now Syracuse was just hoping to get out of the Civic Center with a victory. In 1989, Cliff Robinson scored 24 and Phil Gamble 21 to lead UConn to a 68–62 defeat of the Orangemen in Hartford.

This time around, fifth-ranked Syracuse brought in a formidable front line of 6'10" Derrick Coleman, the Big East's pre-season player of the year, 6'9" Billy Owens, and 6'10" LeRon Ellis. The backcourt featured Stephen Thompson, the team's top returning scorer. The Orangemen wanted to use their big bodies on the Huskies early, trying to take advantage of their distinct size advantage. The Huskies had just two starters over 6'6", Sellers (6'9") and Henefeld (6'7½"). And when Billy Owens followed his own miss and scored, it seemed Syracuse's plan might work.

But two major factors helped the Huskies to build a big lead in the first half. The play of UConn guards Chris Smith and Tate George was better than at any other point in the season. When Smith buried a three-pointer midway through the first half, it gave the Huskies a 16-point lead. George and Smith scored 19 of UConn's first-half total of 38 points.

The second factor for UConn's lead was its three-point shooting. After hitting just 1 of 3 in the first half against Villanova and Pittsburgh, and only 1 of 4 in the first half against Seton Hall, UConn buried 6 of 9 in the first half against Syracuse. Henefeld led UConn with 3 in the half; George added 2.

The magic of the three-point shot is almost hypnotic, with a reaction similar to that of Pavlov's experiment. At the Civic Center, though, there would be no drooling, just wild screams of near hysteria. The crowd yelled, stood, and chanted. With just under ten minutes gone in the first half, UConn was demolishing a team that at one time was number one in the nation, picked to finish second in the conference, and whose coach expected to go to the Final Four. And all of this on national television.

The Huskies took a 38–31 advantage into the locker room, and the Connecticut fans were hopeful. Longtime fans of Connecticut basketball have learned to be able to hope and dream, and to accept. If the 1989–90 Huskies accomplished anything, they taught Connecticut basketball fans that their dreams could come true, and they no longer had to accept losing. They also taught them how to celebrate.

But with another half to play, no one was celebrating yet. Thanks to Connecticut turnovers, second-shot opportunities yielded, and poor UConn shooting in the second half, the Orange came storming back. If the Huskies were going to contend for the Big East crown, they would have to survive runs like these.

Syracuse trimmed the UConn lead to 61–57. When the Orangemen gained possession once more, they looked to go to one of their big men, but George had other ideas. His steal and ensuing basket sparked a 9–2 UConn run, and gave the Huskies a 70–59 victory.

Syracuse's 49–36 domination on the boards was offset by its 29.7 percent shooting in the second half and 35.2 percent for the game. The UConn defense managed 10 more steals, 4 by Henefeld. The "Gaza Stripper" also had 11 points and 7 rebounds in thirty-six minutes of action.

Smith and George paced UConn with 17 points each, with George adding 5 assists. The Huskies got by without a real impact from their bench. DePriest had 9 points, but Cyrulik and Gwynn combined for just 6 more. Murray Williams scored only 2 points on the night, but contributed 5 key assists.

Connecticut fans left ecstatic that night, but in the back of their minds they knew Georgetown was coming.

The Hoyas waltzed into town having won their

UConn cheerleaders react along with 16,294 frenzied fans at the Hartford Civic Center after the Huskies explode to a 14–0 first half lead over Georgetown, prompting a Hoyas time-out.

first twelve games. Georgetown, which whipped the Huskies, 70–58, in Hartford a year earlier, was back and better than before. With a more mature Alonzo Mourning, along with a new-found scorer in Dikembe Mutombo, the Hoyas were out to make UConn victim number thirteen.

Meanwhile, UConn was gunning for a school-record fifth straight conference victory, and with it the opportunity to move into third place in the conference. A spot in the AP poll was also awaiting. The Hoyas were already ranked number two and ready to assume the top spot; number-one Kansas had suffered its first loss that afternoon. For now, Georgetown was the only remaining undefeated team in the nation.

Once again the Civic Center was filled to the rafters. The UConn fans, as they always do at the beginning of a half, stood and clapped in unison until the Huskies scored their first hoop. Once the Huskies scored, they sat down. They got right back up on their feet after UConn darted out to a 14–0 lead and Georgetown called time-out. The din was positively deafening.

Hoyas coach John Thompson said afterward "[UConn's] defensive pressure in the beginning set the tempo of the game." But the visitors were hardly out of the game. Their charge began with an uncontested Mourning slam for Georgetown's first points, 6:06 into the game. Later in the half,

Nadav Henefeld, shooting over two Georgetown defenders, was red hot against the Hoyas. He paced the Huskies to a 70–65 victory with a team-high 21 points, including 5 of 7 from three-point territory.

Tate George is unable to get off a last-second shot before the buzzer, but the Huskies still led, 35–29, at the half.

The high-flying Chris Smith fast-breaks to the hoop, while Rod Sellers trails.

Dwayne Bryant hit a three-pointer to cap a 20–5 run and give the Hoyas a 1-point lead. The UConn fans were stunned, but they continued cheering heartily for the Huskies. George gave UConn the lead back at 21–19 by sinking two free throws. The Huskies then dug in and took a 6-point lead into the second half, 35–29.

UConn came out hot in the second half, but Mark Tillmon's 14 points kept the Hoyas close. Henefeld countered with 14 second-half points of his own.

Henefeld was at his all-purpose best in this game. He played thirty-five minutes and scored a career-high 21 points—15 on three-point shots—and added 5 rebounds, 5 assists, and, of course, 5 steals. Henefeld's court vision, combined with his international basketball experience, was making the Huskies a better club than anyone had expected.

Henefeld's part in the UConn season was unknown in November. He did not even practice with the team before the Marathon Oil game because his SAT scores had yet to be received. After making a statement in small ways through the first seventeen games, Henefeld had definitely made the grade. What made him so intriguing was that even the people that followed the team did not know what aspect of UConn's game he would contribute to most. The love affair between the state's citizens and this young man from Israel was about to begin.

While Henefeld neutralized Tillmon, Mourning consistently dominated the inside for Georgetown. He would finish with 21 points and 12 rebounds. Bryant scored 14 and Tillmon 19, giving the trio all but 11 of Georgetown's points for the game. The UConn defense was once again doing its job.

The Huskies forced the mighty Hoyas into 22 turnovers, while stealing the ball from them 14 times. Smith and George each had 11 points and 4 assists, while Smith added 4 steals and George 3. George also passed the 1,000-point plateau for his career.

Still, the Hoyas had one run left. With 31.9 seconds to play in the game, Tillmon launched a three to cut UConn's lead to 67–65. Thompson then ordered his team to foul. Gwynn was soon fouled by Tillmon, and with the Civic Center

Alonzo Mourning (33) makes Sellers alter his delivery of this shot. Mourning blocked 4 shots to go with his 21 points.

also good, and as the ball fell to the court the Civic Center began to vibrate once again.

After a time-out, Tillmon put up a shot that bounced off the backboard, and DePriest secured the rebound. He was fouled and hit one free throw to put the wraps on a 70–65 victory. As soon as the final buzzer sounded, fans at courtside rushed the floor. It looked as if UConn had just won the Big East championship.

This thunderous Sellers dunk goes uncontested.

crowd silent, Gwynn looked to the fans and pumped his fists in the air. He had already had an outstanding game, scoring 13 points in fifteen minutes of work. Now he accepted support from his teammates and stepped to the line. Gwynn launched the first shot. Good. If he could convert the bonus, it would be difficult for the Hoyas to come back. The next free throw was

The fallout from the Georgetown and Syracuse games was more than just great celebrations and even greater expectations. UConn was 15–3, 5–2 in arguably the best conference in the nation. The Huskies were third behind Georgetown (13–1, 4–1) and St. John's (15–3, 5–1). It was conceivable that UConn could be leading the Big East halfway through the campaign.

UConn? First place in the Big East? Who did these Huskies think they were? Didn't anyone remind them they were supposed to finish eighth in the conference, and that they lost two double-

Mourning again displays his impressive reach as Tate George hangs in the air.

Lyman DePriest finishes yet another break-away for the Huskies.

digit scorers and returned none? There was nothing wrong with the Big East; UConn was merely a young team that did not care who the opposition was. Calhoun ingrained in his players that if they executed the game plan, they could win. The cockiness that goes with being young and talented helped to make UConn a winner of five conference games in a row. And, of course, there was the Huskies' havoc-wreaking defense, which had forced 110 turnovers and stolen the ball 76 times during the streak.

But was UConn really this good? As Calhoun said, "You're not going to beat two of the top five teams in America, both of whom had been number one, unless you're good. You might beat

John Gwynn drives left on Georgetown's Sam Jefferson. Gwynn's clutch scoring punch was especially noteworthy in this contest. Two of his 15 points came on a pair of free throws he hit late in the game to put it out of reach.

one in an upset, but you're not going to beat both." Come Monday, January 22, the Huskies would rejoin the ranks of the Top Twenty as the number twenty team in the nation. "I think for Connecticut it is probably good from the aspect of the fans. There are those who take a lot of joy and pride in the school, and it's the small things that they are cognizant of," Calhoun said. For the fans it was a sign of respect. Staying in the poll would give Connecticut some national acclaim. Dropping from it quickly, as UConn did in 1988–89, would not only be a disappointment for the fans, but the Huskies would be labeled as

a team that could not handle the pressure.

Next for UConn was a January 24 game against Central Connecticut. It would be the Huskies' last game in the thirty-five-year history of the Field House. Then three days later, amidst all of this Husky hysteria, Connecticut would christen its $28 million Gampel Pavilion against St. John's. There would be 8,241 screaming fans in a brand-new curiosity, two nationally ranked teams, and revenge on the minds of all UConn supporters. It figured to be an unforgettable January evening.

Chapter 12

Goodbye to the Old, Hello to the New

January 24, 27, 1990

Throughout the 1989–90 UConn season the phrase "this is the biggest game in UConn history" was muttered by everyone from broadcasters to fans. The win over Georgetown at the Civic Center was certainly special; Calhoun called it the biggest since he'd come to UConn. Even bigger than UConn's NIT title victory. Even though the NIT was significant in its own way and special to the people around UConn at the time, the NCAA championship is the ultimate goal of every Division I school in the nation. And after eighteen games UConn appeared to be a contender.

The Huskies looked to extend their winning streak to six against Central Connecticut State. The Blue Devils were, on paper, no real threat to upset the Huskies. They had finished 10–18 the year before, and in 1989–90 the only teams they would play from high-caliber conferences were UConn and Southern California.

Despite the obvious mismatch, this game was a "can't-miss" for the longtime UConn fan, because it was the finale for Storrs Field House. In a season of unprecedented achievements, it was fitting that this was the year that the school closed the doors to the Field House and christened a new building.

The UConn program began in 1901 as Connecticut Agriculture College basketball. *The Lookout,* UConn's monthly school newspaper at the turn of the century, gave the first insight into basketball at the college. With snow on the ground during one night in January 1901, the CAC's team took a sleigh ride to Willimantic High School. "To the honor of our team it may be said that the students, the young ladies especially, took enough interest in the boys in blue and white jerseys to accompany them to Willimantic to cheer lustily the entire game," the paper reported. There was enthusiasm for Connecticut basketball even in its humble beginnings. UConn defeated the high school team 17–12 for victory number one.

After fourteen years of playing their home games in the Old Main, the school's multipurpose facility (it was a dance hall, chapel, and gymnasium), the team moved into Hawley Armory for its third of five regular games in 1915.

Nadav Henefeld brings the ball up court for the Huskies with Central Connecticut's Marc Rybczyk in pursuit. Converting steals into scoring opportunities is Henefeld's trademark.

CAC downed the Emeralds of William to open the building. In 1916, its first full season in the Armory, CAC won its first three games at home. But the fourth home game, against Rhode Island, was delayed for over a month because of an outbreak of scarlet fever.

The team was known as UConn when it prepared to open another building in 1946–47. The university scheduled all of the home games at the end of the season so the team could play in the Cage, but adverse weather conditions forced UConn to wait until the next season to open the Cage with a 63–29 victory over Maine. The Cage

would eventually become the school's ROTC building, and the team would move from the 3,000-seat facility into the Field House.

The Field House was christened by an outstanding team coached by Hugh Greer. The 1954–55 Huskies finished 20–5 and made the NIT with the help of such players as Art Quimby, UConn's all-time leading rebounder, Gordon Ruddy, and Jim Ahearn. In time UConn outgrew the 4,660-seat Field House, and beginning in 1975 they moved several games to the Hartford Civic Center.

The Huskies joined the Big East in its inaugural season (1979–80) and played part of their conference schedule at the Field House. But in 1986 conference officials called the building aged, and asked UConn to replace it. All Big East games were moved to Hartford as UConn began a fundraising campaign for a new complex. The idea for a new on-campus facility had begun in 1975, but not until 1986 were the plans finalized.

UConn President John Casteen III approached Harry A. Gampel, a 1943 UConn graduate, to help raise money for the new complex. Gampel, who built a multi-million-dollar fortune in construction in Florida and Connecticut, donated $1 million to the project, thus ending the speculation about choosing a name for the building. Rising construction costs delayed the opening of the Pavilion and increased the price tag by $6 million, to $28 million. In addition to Gampel's donation, $7 million came from private sources, and $900,000 came from student fees. The state of Connecticut kicked in $19 million as well. The Pavilion had been scheduled to open in March or April of 1990, but was ready earlier, just in time to coincide with the streaking 1989–90 Huskies. Was it just a simple coincidence? No one knows for sure, but it made for some interesting basketball hysteria.

Amidst all of the excitement there was some sad news. Murray Williams would not be with the team for the last game in the Field House and the opener in the Gampel Pavilion because of the death of his father. Williams had been the Huskies' starting forward the last four games.

Before moving into Gampel, the Huskies had to officially move out of the Field House. Central was determined to spoil the party, but UConn began the game with a 13-2 run. However, Central got back in the contest, pulling as close as 31-29. Then UConn's Smith hit a three-pointer to trigger an 8-0 run. The Huskies took a 47-33 lead into the locker room.

During the break, the 1954-55 UConn team that opened the Field House was welcomed. That era was certainly memorable for followers of Connecticut basketball. But there was no doubting that this 1989-90 team was special in its own way.

The Huskies came out in the second half and put the game out of sight with a 7-0 run. Smith electrified the crowd once again with his fourth three-pointer of the game. With the lead at 54-33, UConn's bench helped to wear down the Central starters. The Huskies' final margin was 99-77.

Ten players scored in double figures, five from each team. For UConn, Smith had 19 points, George 16, Sellers 14, and Henefeld 13 points. John Gwynn scored 12 points and hit the final

Central's Kevin Swann is cut off from the basket by Tate George. The 100–37 Husky victory was the last game that the four-year starter (and the Connecticut team) would play in Storrs Field House.

Scott Burrell (24) gets caught in the net reaching for this rebound as Henefeld (40) and Dan Cyrulik (55) also try to grab the ball.

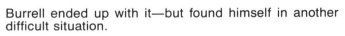

Burrell ended up with it—but found himself in another difficult situation.

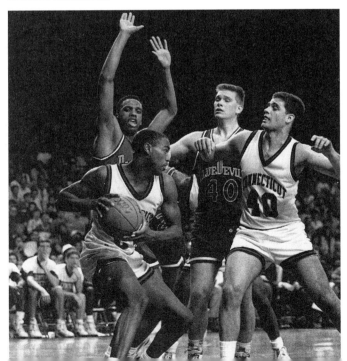

Somehow, though, he manages to get off a clear shot.

basket in the Field House. And Scott Burrell celebrated his return from January 8 knee surgery by scoring 9 points and dishing off 6 assists in twenty-six minutes.

The Huskies ended their stay in the Field House with a 282–85 record (.768 winning percentage), including a 63–7 slate since joining the Big East Conference. For those who attended a

UConn game in the Field House, they take with them certain memories. Calhoun, who also played against UConn in the building, remembers the Virginia Commonwealth game in 1988. The 72–61 win sent the Huskies to the NIT final four and eventually the championship. "We had 9,000 people in there. It was the night the dust came off the rafters," he said. "It is one of the greatest stories of fan enthusiasm I had ever heard. That is why I am never surprised at the way our fans react."

New memories were waiting to happen at the Pavilion. St. John's entered the opening game at Gampel with a 17–3 overall record and a 6–1 mark in the conference. Georgetown would lose to Syracuse that same night, so a Husky win would put them in a tie with St. John's for the Big East lead.

UConn fans had to wonder who would stop St. John's Jayson Williams and "Boo" Harvey, who combined for 45 points against UConn earlier in the season. They could barely wait to find out; alumni, students, and Husky fans in general converged on the Pavilion the afternoon of the game. They wanted to see what all the hysteria was about.

The opening night was as heralded in the Storrs community as a major motion picture release is in Hollywood. Legislators and high-ranking university officials were in attendance. The students, who had begun their spring semester five days earlier, would have a Big East game on campus. They would occupy the two top sections behind the baskets and a majority of the seats in the lower level behind the baskets. More than 3,000 of the 8,241 seats would be occupied by students.

"It's great to have all the fans and alumni and I really appreciate them," Calhoun said. "But from a coaching standpoint there is nothing better than knowing that you have 3,000 students here making this an event and giving them pride in their university."

UConn's former athletic director, John Toner, was the man responsible for the Gampel Pavilion, Calhoun said. "This is his very own building." Toner had insisted that the Pavilion be located across from the library and a brief walk from the Student Union. The Pavilion was also

no more than a ten-minute walk from all the dorms on campus. Said Calhoun, "We wanted to get the students involved. The students walk through here all day long. It's in the center of campus, not that it is the most important building on campus, but it's a nice diversion and it's a place that unifies the student body."

UConn could have used a bit of unifying at the time. At the outset of the spring semester, the campus had come under the specter of some

Toraino Walker logged sixteen minutes of playing time against the Blue Devils—crucial minutes to prepare for important games down the stretch.

A sellout crowd of dedicated fans help UConn break in Harry A. Gampel Pavilion versus the Redmen of St. John's.

racial tensions. Tuition was going up again, and a deficit in the state budget resulted in cuts for the school. UConn's engineering school was close to losing its accreditation because of inadequate funding. Bricks from the library were practically falling off, and as a result of the budget cuts hours were reduced at the Homer Babbidge Library. The basketball team would serve as a diversion and a sense of school pride for the students who would eventually speak out about these problems.

The students came out en masse the Monday before the game. More than 4,000 waited in line just to get a lottery ticket. The 1,000 or so with winning tickets would be able to buy just two tickets each to the game. Others who wanted to avoid the lottery had bought season tickets just to make sure they were part of this historical event.

Fans began lining up in front of the Pavilion doors three hours before tip-off. Inside the building in the Founders Club, program sup-

porters and distinguished guests such as Gov. William O'Neill awaited the start of the game. The governor, like many others in the state, was fast becoming a Husky hoop fanatic.

Five UConn students were the first outside the building. Keith Kasner, Ted Young, Dennis Lynch, John Heine, and Ron Beasley had blue and white paint on their faces and their chests, which spelled out "U-C-O-N-N#1". An hour later, the chant of "Open the doors" rang out from the approximately 200 fans who had gathered early. The crowd grew a bit larger, and at 6:30 p.m. the Harry A. Gampel Pavilion was opened.

The student sections filled up first. Minutes after the doors opened, these enthusiastic students would be chanting "Let's go Huskies" at the top of their lungs. The blue-and-white tapestry of screaming humanity was in effect a chorus testing the acoustics of this playground.

While the students screamed and chanted, the lower levels began to fill up with alumni, donors, and season ticket-holders. The Wave began in the upper reaches of the building. Portions of the lower levels participated, and those that did not were booed.

Michael Ponte was one such student that was taking in the moment. "This is better than any ten-keg party," he professed, while sitting with his friends two rows from the top of the Pavilion. Ponte wore his good-luck red and blue sweater; he said the Huskies had never lost while he was wearing it. To the students' backs, on the wall under the scoreboard and centered between the American and Connecticut state flags, was a banner with the gravestones of Pittsburgh, Villanova, Seton Hall, Syracuse, and Georgetown. They had hoped to add St. John's to the list, but arena officials made sure the banner was not around by the end of the game.

Chris Smith drives toward the lane against Jason Buchanan while the rest of the Redmen try to get back on defense. Again, Smith led UConn to victory (72–58) with 20 points.

Cyrulik turned in a solid performance against St. John's with 13 key points off the bench.

Keith Furniss, a UConn student, gave Gampel Pavilion rave reviews. "When you come here you are more in awe of this than the Field House. This is a real place to play," he said. Furniss added that he hoped UConn would not spoil the opening night with a loss.

Jim Calhoun, Howie Dickenman, Dave Leitao, and Glen Miller, the UConn coaching staff, followed the team out on the floor less than eight minutes before game time. The ovation they received was nothing less than thunderous. UConn student Caroline Daly sang the national anthem, and then Roger Baker gave goose bumps to the UConn faithful with one sentence: "Welcome, ladies and gentlemen, to the Harry A. Gampel Pavilion for the return of Big East basketball to the UConn campus."

Gov. O'Neill made the ceremonial ball toss.

He then took his seat next to UConn President John Casteen III, nine rows from the court. Both team's lineups were announced. Henefeld received an extra-loud ovation after earning Big East co-player of the week honors (with Eric Murdock of Providence). Henefeld was the first freshman ever to receive the award.

The officials Larry Lembo, Ted Valentine, and Tom Corbin readied the two squads for the center jump, and the fans rose to their feet; that included the donors and alumni in the well-tailored suits and elegant dresses and the students with the painted faces. Even the governor was standing and cheering as UConn readied for one of its biggest games of the season. The ball was tossed in the air, and Tate George controlled the tip for the Huskies. The fans would not stop cheering, even after St. John's Robert Werdann put in the first points in Gampel history. The screaming peaked when UConn's Rod Sellers scored on the next trip down court.

Chris Smith and Burrell prevented the first half from being a rerun of the Huskies' earlier trip to St. John's. They scored all but 10 of UConn's 35 points. Smith hit on 3 three-pointers in the last 2:48, the last one a buzzer-beater that gave UConn a 35–34 halftime lead. "We were down and then I hit that three and we went into the locker room all pumped up," Smith said later. "We came out for the second half ready to play."

Burrell, for one, was ready. When the 6'5" forward left the UConn lineup because of surgery on January 8, UConn was 0–2 in the Big East. In this, his first Big East game back, people joked that Burrell would be a jinx. He effectively dispelled that claim by scoring 12 points on 5 of 7 shooting. And when he needed support, Calhoun was there for the freshman. After Burrell sailed an outlet pass over George's head, Calhoun called out "Scott." When Burrell looked back the coach clapped his hands as if to say, "Let's go." This sign of confidence showed the next time down court as Burrell soared above the crowd on the floor and jammed home Smith's alley-oop pass. Instant fan-demonium.

The game's back-and-forth flow, though, kept the audience in suspense most of the night. But with the score tied at 51, the Huskies made their

Head Coach Jim Calhoun discusses UConn's win over St. John's in a post-game press conference. The victory put UConn in a tie with St. John's atop the Big East.

its impressive old self. The Huskies forced 16 turnovers on the night and collect 10 more steals. Through the season's first twenty games UConn led the Big East in forcing turnovers (428) and stealing the ball (278).

St. John's Boo Harvey hit a three with 2:10 to play, cutting UConn's lead to 61–54. Redmen coach Lou Carnesecca, in an attempt to set up his defense, called a time-out. What he failed to realize was that his team had called its final time-out two minutes earlier. A technical foul was assessed, and UConn extended its lead to 63–54. This started a 9–4 Husky run that wrapped up the 72–58 victory.

As the final buzzer sounded, the noise once again threatened to blow off the Gampel dome. UConn, the team picked to finish eighth in the Big East, now shared the top rung with St. John's— ahead of Syracuse and Georgetown. The Huskies did it with defense again, limiting the Redmen to 26.7 percent shooting in the second half. Calhoun said, "For the first time in a while we had to suck it up a little bit. We couldn't just steal the ball and get an awful lot of layups."

Smith paced the Huskies with 20 points. Thirty-eight of UConn's 72 points came from the bench, making up for lackluster offensive showings by starters Sellers and Lyman DePriest (2 points each). Henefeld had just 4 points but continued to show his versatility by dishing off for 5 assists and making 4 steals. Henefeld's final steal gave him 91 on the season, breaking the NCAA freshman record set by Providence's Murdock in 1987–88. And Henefeld still had ten regular-season games and the Big East and NCAA tournaments to go.

At the conclusion of the game, as the P.A. announcer, Roger Baker, told the crowd that UConn was tied for first place in the Big East, Calhoun pointed to the screaming students. "It's the students that really appreciate our effort," he said afterwards. "I was telling the students, 'Hey, it's you guys.' And it really was."

The Huskies had just avenged one of their worst beatings in recent memory. They also had seventeen victories, the mark they had always seemed to miss during the season. It became clear that UConn would not miss this season's NCAA tournament.

most important run to date. This time Gwynn and Cyrulik came off the bench to spark the Huskies. They began a 10–0 run when Henefeld stole the ball and dished off to Cyrulik for a 53–51 lead. Gwynn and Cyrulik combined for 7 points in the spurt and 24 of UConn's 37 points in the second half. Both finished with 13 points.

As Gwynn and Cyrulik poured in the points, the UConn press, a.k.a. the "steal curtain," was

Chapter 13

. . . Eight, Nine, Ten

January 30, February 3, 6, 1990

After the dust had settled and the Pavilion's rafters had stopped shaking, the Huskies found themselves entering a new era of Connecticut basketball. On Monday, Jan. 29, 1990, the Associated Press poll placed the Huskies number thirteen. This ranking was the highest ever for a UConn team. This alone was reason to celebrate, but this year the celebrations came in waves. On that same evening St. John's fell to Syracuse, 70–65, giving UConn sole possession of first place with a conference record of 6–2.

Georgetown (No. 6) and Syracuse (No. 7) still were ahead of the Huskies in the AP poll, if not the Big East standings. That didn't bother Calhoun at all. "It's not that I don't like the AP poll, I just think it's not of great significance," he said. "I don't think it really shows who your best teams are." Calhoun admitted the national exposure couldn't really hurt, but that appearing in the poll week after week could get burdensome.

There was one other point Calhoun continually stressed. "I don't want to be judged as a coach in what we do in a game, five games, or even a season. See what we've done here in four years—see who has graduated, see what kind of kids we have in the program, see how they handle the press—that's what I want to be evaluated on. I'm not a sprint runner, I'm more of a marathon runner."

And at the halfway point of UConn's 1989–90 marathon, Calhoun would confess, "We are not that good of a team. We don't shoot well." If UConn had a problem, it was indeed its shooting. In their first twenty games, the Huskies had hit on 45.2 percent of their field goals, and only 41 percent in Big East play. Their three-point shooting was probably a little above average at 35.9 percent, and their free-throw shooting was a bit below at 61.0 percent.

Then how could this team have been 17–3? Defense was not the only answer. For one, the Huskies were averaging 4 more rebounds a game than their opponents. UConn also had five players scoring in double figures: Henefeld, George, Sellers, Gwynn, and Smith (team-leading 15.9 points per game). The Huskies were averaging 79 points a game, 6 more than the

UConn sets up its trademark full court pressure defense against UMass. As it did all year, the defense eventually wore down the opponent, recording 13 team steals against the Minutemen.

1988–89 team that had high-scoring Cliff Robinson and Phil Gamble.

Defense, though, spelled success for the Huskies. The steals and forced turnovers had translated to 219 more UConn shots than the opposition. As a result they had 135 more field goals. And the defense was holding foes to 64.3 points per game. "We just feed off each other," Calhoun said. "We believe in ourselves, and it is important for a team to believe that they can do well."

The Huskies took their eight-game winning streak to Massachusetts on January 30. The 4,024 enthusiastic Minutemen fans crammed into Curry Hicks Cage, and UMass 20-points-a-game scorer Jim McCoy figured to make UConn's task difficult.

Sure enough, with under four minutes left in the first half the Minutemen held a three-point lead. They were handling the UConn press, and the Cage crazies smelled the same kind of upset that UConn had scored against Georgetown and Syracuse. However, Scott Burrell came off the Husky bench with other ideas. He scored all 7 of his first-half points in the last three minutes, giving the visitors a 37–33 halftime lead.

Burrell continued his domination at the outset of the second half. He scored on a layup, was fouled in the process, and hit the free throw for a 40–33 UConn lead. Seconds later, as the Minutemen tried to work the ball up the court, Henefeld stepped into the passing lane and picked off yet another pass. The forward then found George for a six-foot jumper that ex-

UMass holds on to a slim lead as Nadav Henefeld puts up a finger roll from close range. Scott Burrell soon came off the UConn bench to erase Massachusetts' lead with 7 quick points.

tended the lead to nine, just fifty-eight seconds into the half.

The Huskies' torrid shooting continued throughout the second half; they hit at a 67.7 percent clip (21 for 31) en route to a 94–75 victory. Smith paced UConn with 22 points. George contributed 16 points, 12 assists, and 8 rebounds. Burrell scored 14 while Henefeld and Gwynn added 11 each. It was becoming painfully clear to the opposition that this UConn team, unlike previous ones, had many weapons.

UMass was not a Syracuse or a Georgetown, but its home-court edge rivaled any team's. "Their fans were the sixth man on the court. But I think we did a good job of overcoming that," Gwynn said.

While the 18–3 Huskies were beating UMass, Georgetown downed Seton Hall to pull even with UConn at 6–2 in the conference. The Huskies' next road test was at Providence, where they had not won since 1984. In the last five years, UConn was 3–8 against the Friars.

Providence was 12–6 with ten regular-season games to go. If the Friars were going to make a return trip to the NCAA tournament they would have to play at least .500 ball in that span. A victory over UConn would certainly impress the tournament's selection committee, and it would put the Friars merely a half-game behind the Huskies in the conference standings.

The key for UConn would be to neutralize Providence's potent backcourt of Carlton Screen and Eric Murdock. Thus far the Huskies were averaging a conference-best 13.8 steals a game. Henefeld led the way with 4.5 per game.

Buses filled with UConn fans pulled up to the Providence Civic Center. The rabid fans did not go unnoticed; in fact, they angered some of the Providence faithful. Even before the game this match-up had the possibility of being a Big East classic.

St. John's had failed to beat Georgetown earlier in the day, so UConn needed a win to remain tied with the Hoyas for first place. Providence played the Huskies tight for the first six minutes. The visitors led 15–14 when they went on a 29–7 tear. Providence fell apart, turning the ball over 12 times and sending UConn to the line 21 times in the half. Six of those op-

Tate George powers his way to the glass as the Huskies open up a comfortable lead early in the second half against UMass.

portunities came from three Providence technical fouls. The Huskies hit on 14 of the free throws while Providence went just 3 of 9 from the line.

UConn led 46–28 at halftime and was on its way to consecutive victory number nine. The Huskies built the cushion without sinking a three-point shot. The 13,160 home team fans in the Civic Center were stunned and vented their frustrations on the referees.

Providence came out better prepared for the second half, whittling the lead to 11 with 13:39 to go. UConn led by 13 later in the half when Murdock was called for a technical foul after he got too aggressive underneath the basket. This ignited the Huskies to a 13–4 run that gave them an 88–66 lead with 1:50 to play. The final score was 92–77 as Providence became UConn's seventh straight, and different, Big East victim.

It was the most points ever registered by a UConn team in a Big East game. Smith showed the way with 24 points. Williams returned to the starting lineup and scored 6 points in seventeen minutes of play. Gwynn added 15 off the bench. Henefeld had no steals but still managed 12 points.

Connecticut's bench starts the celebration as the Huskies cruise to a 94–75 win over Massachusetts.

Henefeld was no longer a mystery man. Clearly becoming the most dominant freshman in the conference, he made his network television debut (CBS) during the halftime of the St. John's–Georgetown game. The feature opened with war footage from the Middle East; later Henefeld was shown as an Israeli soldier. He was not pleased with the way he was depicted in the piece, but Henefeld is the type of person who is not bothered by such distractions. The twenty-one-year-old showed he was mature enough to concentrate on his job at hand, and as a result he earned Big East rookie-of-the-week honors for the second time.

Burrell cooled off a little following his offensive spurt against UMass, but still contributed some quality minutes. He and Smith (right) close in on Friars' star Carlton Screen.

Chris Smith turns in another big performance with a game-high 24 points against the Providence Friars.

The impressive victory over Providence propelled UConn into the Top Ten for the first time ever. In fact, the Huskies were eighth in the AP poll. In the Big East they were 7–2 and tied for first with Georgetown, a game ahead of Syracuse.

The Huskies were after victory number twenty when Fairfield visited the Pavilion Tuesday, February 6. A UConn team had not won twenty regular-season games since 1964–65, when the Huskies went 23–3 and made the NCAA tournament. There was no doubt about UConn being invited to this year's dance.

UConn did not look like a tournament team, however, in the first half against Fairfield. Ed Duncan led the Stags to an early 11–4 lead. The

Henefeld pumps a short jumper as Screen tries to draw an offensive foul.

Providence's Chris Watts does his best not to foul John Gwynn as the Huskies' valuable sixth man goes in for a layup. Gwynn scored 15 of UConn's team record 92 points in a Big East game.

Fairfield gave Connecticut all it wanted in the first half, including this Drew Henderson rejection of a George shot attempt.

stunned UConn crowd was soon revived as the Huskies forced 4 consecutive turnovers to key a 7-0 run.

The Huskies created 13 first-half turnovers, but their lead at halftime was just 28-23. UConn had not scored that few points in a half since the first half of its December loss to Villanova. Poor shooting haunted the Huskies again; they shot 36.4 percent from the floor.

Calhoun said of the first half, "Fairfield dictated the tempo; we had a real tough time. We quick-shot for the first time in a while. We were trying to get it over with in the first few minutes, and that doesn't work in basketball." The coach likely gave his players a more graphic account, because they came out of the locker room as though they were facing Georgetown or Syracuse.

Fairfield took possession of the ball at the start of the second half, and the Huskies immediately forced a five-second violation. UConn then rattled off 10 straight points, 7 by George. Said Calhoun, "We came out and made a commitment that we were going to play defense, Connecticut style."

The Huskies built the lead to 39-25, and then Henefeld scored 8 of their next 9 points, the final 2 coming off his 98th steal of the season. He

Toraino Walker experienced his share of problems, too; here he disputes a call by the referee.

Smith lofts a ten-footer in a crowded lane. The Huskies would eventually get on track and blow out Fairfield, 74-39.

eventually finished with 18 points. The final score was UConn 74, Fairfield 39. The Huskies converted 24 Fairfield turnovers into 25 points; they also added 15 steals to their season total. The defense also limited the Stags to 5 of 20 shooting in the second half. UConn bounced back to hit 54.3 percent of its shots in the second half.

The next night, Georgetown beat Pitt to take sole possession of first place in the Big East. UConn's next conference game was Saturday at sixth-ranked Syracuse. The Orangemen didn't figure to shoot 35 percent and score 59 points once again, as they had one month earlier in Hartford.

Chapter 14

UConn Came,
UConn Couldn't
February 10, 13, 1990

The Carrier Dome in Syracuse, New York, is easily the largest on-campus facility in the nation. More than 30,000 maniacs routinely flock to the Dome—four times the number who watch UConn in Gampel Pavilion—to see the Orangemen. And on February 10, Syracuse shattered its own NCAA on-campus attendance record.

A throng of 32,820 filled the Carrier Dome to see if their Orange could end UConn's ten-game win streak. Said Calhoun, "Syracuse is treating this like a game versus Georgetown."

Following its January loss to UConn, Syracuse dropped a 87–86 decision to Providence in the Carrier Dome. At that point, Syracuse coach Jim Boeheim made a change in his starting backcourt, replacing David Johnson with freshman Michael Edwards. Edwards proceeded to average 5.6 assists a game and help Syracuse win its next five. "Michael Edwards has helped them to distribute the ball better," Calhoun said. "He keys the play of Stevie [Thompson], Derrick [Coleman], and Billy [Owens]." The trio each had averaged over 17 points a game during the streak.

UConn's defense was fast becoming the talk of college basketball. How could a team with such young and relatively small players execute a system so well? One reason was Rod Sellers, who had started every UConn game thus far. The sophomore didn't get the media attention, but he was a steady performer averaging 10 points and 5.7 rebounds. The Huskies, led by Henefeld's 6.1 per game, were averaging 40.2 rebounds a contest.

But the Orangemen fans were ready to take the bite out of the Huskies. They wore buttons that read "UConn, UCame, UCouldn't." And the Orange appeared bent on delivering an early knockout. They led 11–0 with just 2:28 gone in the game. Syracuse was on its way to 58.1 percent field-goal shooting in the first half.

The Huskies' bench got them back in the game. Burrell hit a pair of three-pointers, and Gwynn fired in three more to cut the deficit to single digits. Gwynn led all first-half scorers with 13 points; teammate Smith was shut out.

With the lead down to seven, 36–29, Smith grabbed a rebound and found Burrell streaking to the basket. Burrell soared for the alley-oop pass, but it sailed out of reach and Burrell was left holding the rim. A technical foul was assessed and Coleman hit the two free throws. Syracuse then got the ball back, and Owens nailed a three off the inbounds pass. What could have been a five-point lead now was 41–29. It was a sequence that could have changed the course of the UConn season, but this team was not going to rely on fate for its victories. Not yet, anyway.

Syracuse's lead at halftime was 43–31. The Huskies were down primarily because they were 11 for 33 from the floor, while the Orangemen were 5 of 9 from three-point range. This after Boeheim had banned this team from taking the shot a month earlier. Following the game Calhoun would joke, "I want it to be known that Jimmy Boeheim cheated. He said he was going to banish the three-pointer."

Coleman (career-high 29 points) and Owens (21 points) helped Syracuse maintain its double-figure lead in the second half. Coleman's fast-break layup made it 81–66 with less than five minutes to play. But some sharp three-point shooting helped UConn close to 88–82 with 34 seconds to go.

Coleman, looking to end the game perhaps a bit too quickly, sent an outlet pass the length of the court and into the seats to give UConn the ball back. Gwynn immediately was fouled by Edwards and hit both shots to cut the lead to 88–84. Then LeRon Ellis was fouled by DePriest with 23 seconds left. Ellis missed the free throw and UConn controlled the rebound. But Henefeld's three-point attempt bounced harmlessly off the front of the rim, and soon thereafter Ellis sank the clinching free throws. The 90–86 loss was UConn's first in nearly six weeks, and it pushed the team into third place in the Big East.

Their ten-game win streak was history, but the Huskies had shown great courage in nearly overcoming the huge halftime deficit. They scored 55 points in the second half on 53.8 percent shooting, and they made 6 steals and forced 12 turnovers for the game. The comeback helped prove the Huskies' earlier defeat of the Orangemen was no fluke.

After the Huskies slipped to tenth in the AP poll, Calhoun said, "The toughest thing we have had to deal with these past few weeks is [the pressure caused by] the national rankings." The Huskies would attempt to get back on track at Pitt, where they had not won since the 1983–84 season. The seventh-place Panthers had struggled most of the season, but they were coming off a blow-out of Providence, in which they scored 117 points.

The previous night, Villanova had shocked Syracuse, 60–56. It was the Orange's fourth Big East defeat, one more than the Huskies had.

Before the Pitt game, Jim Calhoun told the media they should not center their attention on the rising star, Henefeld. His point was well taken. True, the Huskies would not have been as successful to this point without the forward, who had more than 100 steals, was averaging in double figures in scoring, and was an excellent passer and rebounder. But this was a team, and Calhoun was trying to deflect some of the attention Henefeld was getting. Following the game, there'd be no stopping it.

Calhoun made his first lineup switch in three games, replacing Williams with DePriest. The Huskies entered Fitzgerald Field House knowing they would be facing a sellout of 6,798.

Pitt led, 16–15, midway through the first half when UConn got the break it needed. Henefeld hit a pair of free throws, and in the process Sellers was intentionally fouled by the Panthers' Brian Shorter. Pitt coach Paul Evans vehemently protested the call, and for his trouble received a technical foul. Evans was not quite finished. After a few more words with the referees, Evans earned "T" number two.

Sellers stood alone on the line and, with the frenzied Pitt fans in the background, missed his two free throws. Smith then came to the line to take four technical foul shots. Facing the same situation as Sellers, Smith calmly sank all four shots. The Huskies then got the ball back, and Henefeld connected on a jumper to give the Huskies a 23–16 lead without ever crossing midcourt. The 8-point run would prove to be the game's turning point.

Pittsburgh, though, had cut the lead to three, 38–35, by the break. UConn's Smith didn't miss a shot as he scored 18 points in the half. But it was Henefeld who became UConn's go-to guy in the second half. He eventually finished with a career-high 27 points (9 of 17 from the floor), 5 rebounds, 4 steals, and 4 assists. Smith finished with 22 points.

The Huskies' "steal curtain" defense produced 10 more steals while forcing 20 turnovers. Still, UConn needed two late free throws from Henefeld, who blocked out the rabid fans behind the basket, to wrap up the 80–77 victory. Finally, there was nothing left for Henefeld to accomplish on this night.

Ramat-Hasharon, Israel, is half a world away from the United States and Eastern Connecticut. But beneath the rubble of a tattered land, there remains a special place in the people's hearts for Nadav Henefeld. He is the native son who has gone to play the sport of basketball at an American university.

Henefeld came to UConn after serving the required three years of military service in Israel. He was a stranger in a strange land—gone were his family, his friends, and his native foods. All he knew was that he would be playing basketball, and that pleased him.

Little did Calhoun know how well Henefeld would integrate into his system. His international experience with the Israeli National Team brought a different twist to Connecticut basketball. The fans fell for the newcomer immediately, making his adjustment even easier. Loyal fans flew the Israeli flag at Husky home games and waved it proudly for Nadav. No one could have ever predicted such a warm reception.

Henefeld's adept ability to get in position for steals fit nicely with Calhoun's disruptive defense. It earned him nicknames such as "The Chosen Man from the Promised Land" and the "Gaza Stripper." Gampel Pavilion became the "Dove Dome."

Henefeld was eventually named Big East rookie of the year, leading the conference in steals with 138—second in the nation. He obliterated Bobby Dulin's UConn single-season steal record of 83. That means 138 times Henefeld not only foiled the opponent's attempt to score, but simultaneously created a scoring opportunity for the Huskies.

The Connecticut Jewish community was proud of its countryman. Those who had close ties with their homeland felt a sense of pride, because in a sense Nadav was the surrogate son to whom they could relate. He was asked to speak at numerous Jewish functions in the community and around the state. He obliged for the most part, but due to the time constraints he had with classes and basketball he was unable to fulfill all of them. He received Bar Mitzvah invitations from people he didn't even know. What would happen come tournament time?

UConn's dream season continued with the win at Pitt. "To sweep a quality team like Pitt on a hostile court in a game we could've lost is just an example of how we've been able to handle such pressure," Calhoun said afterward. "We have not been an emotional team all year."

When the Huskies came off the court, they learned Georgetown had dropped its game at Providence. Connecticut and Georgetown now were tied for the lead at 8–3, while Syracuse and St. John's were right behind at 8-4. February was heating up in the Big East.

Chapter 15

Home Court Heroes
February 17, 19, 24, 1990

First place in anything is special. Just ask UConn's Huskies, who sat atop the Big East standings Feb. 13, 1990, after Georgetown's loss to Providence. With five regular-season games to go, and the next three at home, UConn was in prime position for its first-ever Big East championship.

The first step would be against the only Big East team that had escaped the ravaging Huskies thus far: Boston College. The Eagles came into Gampel Pavilion with a conference mark of 1–10. The Eagles were picked to finish ninth in the league, and they were well on their way. Despite a win over Seton Hall and a one-point loss to Villanova in their two games prior to the match-up with the Huskies, BC had lost eight of its other nine Big East matches by at least 10 points.

But this was still a Big East team, a fact Calhoun reiterated before the game. UConn was not about to take the 7–14 Eagles lightly. And 8,302 fans would pack the Pavilion to ensure that the Huskies' sixth man would be heard loud and clear.

With a junior, a sophomore, and three fresh-men in its lineup, BC was perhaps the only team in the league that could make the Huskies look like graybeards. UConn sophomores Henefeld and Smith (Henefeld was declared a sophomore and not a freshman because of his age) looked to continue their hot shooting from Pittsburgh. Another sophomore, Sellers, looked to neutralize BC's Doug Able on the boards.

The Eagles raced out to a quick 14–9 lead, and the game had the look of being a tight one. Then the Huskies got serious. Smith connected on a three-point basket. Williams, who had gone scoreless the last two games, came off the bench to hit a turnaround jumper. On UConn's next possession, Williams dribbled up the court and fired a perfect pass to the streaking Burrell, whose layup gave UConn the lead. Smith would be the next beneficiary of a Williams assist. On a fast break, Williams dished the ball behind his head to Smith for the jam and an 18–14 lead. Williams' spark resulted in a 16–0 run that virtually buried the Eagles. "That was really the Murray Williams of old," Calhoun said afterward.

BC coach Jim O'Brien called a time-out. It

In just seventeen minutes of playing time, John Gwynn led the Huskies in scoring with 18 points (season high) against Boston College.

through the second half to 70–48. BC tried to come back behind the play of Lior Arditti, another native of Israel. A teammate of Henefeld's on the Israeli National Team, Arditti showed he could play this game, too. He connected on 5 three-pointers and finished with 20 points, five more than his countryman Henefeld.

Sellers added 16 points and 9 rebounds for the Huskies. But it was Connecticut's guard play that keyed the 89–67 victory. Smith, George, and Gwynn combined for 47 points, with Gwynn (18) leading the way. "Their backcourt is one of the most underrated in the country," O'Brien said. "I think Smith and George can play with any backcourt around."

Connecticut, though, was being equated with defense. This time the Huskies came up with 12 steals and forced 23 turnovers, and limited BC to 41.4 percent shooting in the second half.

The victory sent another UConn sellout crowd home happy. Since the January 15 game in Hartford against Syracuse, every game UConn had played was a sellout. The BC conquest also gave UConn a win against every team in the Big East, another first for the Huskies. They still shared the conference lead with Georgetown, which defeated Seton Hall on the same evening.

Come Monday the Huskies found themselves ranked sixth nationally, behind Missouri, Kansas, Duke, UNLV, and Georgetown. Where was Syracuse? The Orangemen had dropped two games the past week, to Villanova and to Notre Dame. Meanwhile, the Henefeld story continued as he was named Big East rookie of the week for the third time.

Providence was coming off upsets of St. John's and Georgetown when it visited Gampel Pavilion on Monday, February 19. UConn was after victory number twenty-three, which would tie the record for most wins in school history. The Friars needed the victory to help keep their NCAA hopes alive. The scene was set, and the witnesses would include a national television audience via ESPN.

UConn took control in the first half like most everyone in the building thought it would. The Huskies shot just 39.4 percent, but took eight more shots and hit 11 of 12 free throws and thus led, 39–28, at intermission.

was his first visit to UConn since his days as an assistant coach for the Huskies, and by this time he was probably wishing he hadn't made the trip. George (16 points, 6 assists, 2 steals) buried a three for UConn and then soon after hit two foul shots.

UConn led 25–14 after the run, then held off a BC charge and took an 11-point lead into the break, 43–32. The Huskies' defense was not as impressive as in games past, especially against a team it was supposed to dominate. But UConn's dastardly defense would return in the second half.

Connecticut doubled its halftime lead midway

Nadav "Dove" Henefeld was by now a highly recognized force on this Husky team. He earned his third Big East rookie-of-the-week award following the Boston College game. Through his hustle and level-headed play, he won over the hearts of the UConn fans, too. He will be missed.

A sellout crowd rocks Gampel Pavilion in a tight UConn win over Providence.

At 8:05 to play in the second half, UConn held what seemed like a safe 56–44 lead. However, Providence's Quinton Burton sparked a comeback with a pair of three-pointers, the last coming at 1:29, to cut the UConn lead to 62–61. And the Huskies had not scored a field goal since the eight-minute mark.

After a UConn time-out, George was called for traveling, giving Providence a chance to take the lead. Moments later, Smith committed his fifth foul of the evening, sending Carlton Screen to the foul line. He missed the front end of the one-and-bonus, and Henefeld grabbed the rebound. But the Huskies missed two of three free throws down the stretch, and Providence had a chance to tie. With six seconds left, Carlton Screen shot and missed, but Eric Murdock's follow-up with five seconds to go tied the game at 63 and forced overtime.

The Huskies had blown an 11-point halftime lead by shooting just 28.6 percent (8 of 28) from the floor and 43.8 percent at the line in the second half. After the game Calhoun said, "This is the first time in a while a team made a run at us. They tightened up and played like an emotional team that really wanted the basketball game."

The Friars scored just five seconds into the extra session on two Murdock free throws. One minute later, Henefeld converted a steal into a game-tying layup. For Henefeld, it was just his sixth and seventh points of the game. But his 4 steals and 9 rebounds proved his all-around game was still there.

Murdock gave Providence the lead once again, but then UConn's Chris Smith moved to the forefront. First he contributed a three-point play, followed by a steal and an assist, and, finally, two free throws. When he was finished, UConn had itself a 72–67 lead. But the sophomore soon after fouled out.

Now it was Murdock's turn. He hit two free throws, then canned a three to knot the score at 72 with less than fifty seconds to go. The fans stayed on their feet as UConn held the ball for one last shot. With about five seconds left

Scott Burrell had an all-around game: he scored 12 points, grabbed 7 rebounds and 2 steals, and added a blocked shot (right).

Henefeld launched a three. The ball hit hard against the backboard and bounced straight into the hole. UConn led 75–72, with two seconds left.

The Friars did not even have a chance to attempt one last shot. The cheers rang loud and clear as UConn tucked away its tenth Big East victory and record-tying twenty-third overall. UConn was still in first place.

The Huskies would have a rare four days off before they played their final home game of the season. Georgetown had a chance to rejoin the Huskies atop the Big East, but failed to do so by losing to St. John's at home. Meanwhile, Syracuse moved into a tie for second with the Hoyas. UConn needed two wins in its last three games to clinch at least a tie for the league title.

What a difference one year had made for

Chris Smith sneaks in a shove with his left forearm while trying to block Marques Bragg's shot.

Seton Hall. In 1988–89 the Pirates went 31–7 and came within three seconds of beating Michigan for the national championship. Now, coming into Gampel Pavilion on Saturday, February 24, the Pirates were 11–13 overall and 4–9 in the conference.

The 1989–90 Huskies' rise to national prominence rekindled memories of the 1988–89 Seton Hall team for many. College basketball analyst Dick Vitale noted the similarities. "You see [John] Morton in the backcourt [17.3 points per game] with Gerald Greene [5.1 assists per game], and you see Chris Smith back there [16.6 p.p.g.] with Tate George [5.3 a.p.g.]. You see the excellent bench play with the guy from the foreign land [Henefeld] coming in, à la the same thing with Gaze coming in from Australia." There were other similarities: both played in the Great Alaskan Shootout during their respective seasons, both were picked fairly low in the Big East preseason poll, and both had lost 20 p.p.g. scorers (UConn's Cliff Robinson and Seton Hall's Mark Bryant) to the Portland Trail Blazers. The only clear difference was that Seton Hall's great team was composed of mostly seniors, while UConn had just one senior in Tate George.

Seton Hall was the only hurdle that remained between UConn and Georgetown for a shot at the Big East championship. Before the game the Huskies were aware that Georgetown had ripped Villanova, 88–53. Calhoun and his team had their sights set on the Hoyas and their upcoming match-up. "We put on the board 'Big East Championship.' It was the first time we acknowledged the fact that we probably have a chance," the coach said. "This team is young enough that they are just playing games; I think that is their best attribute." That message on the board would work well as a motivational tool for the Huskies, who came onto the court with a desire to finish this game early.

But first George, the team's only senior, and his family were honored at center court. Calhoun walked out and gave his co-captain a brief hug, because this certainly was not a goodbye. The ovation for George was loud. This was the same player who had been blasted by many of the fans in the past, but once again this was a

Jim Calhoun keeps a watchful eye on a meeting between the referee and Friars' head coach, Rick Barnes.

different season. They applauded George for his dedication to the team, the school-record 119 games he had played in, and the school record 645 assists.

At the start of the game, it appeared the players' minds were elsewhere. The first basket came 2:21 into the contest, a hook shot by Henefeld in the paint. Eight seconds later George turned a Seton Hall turnover into a layup, and immediately thereafter Henefeld

come. Such was rarely the case in the past.

The Pirates got no closer than 19. Smith paced the 79–57 rout with a 21-point performance. Even though this UConn team was just that, a team, Smith had become the definitive scorer. And Henefeld was the consummate handy man; in this game he had 15 points, 6 steals and 5 assists in just twenty-two minutes. George turned his emotional pre-game sendoff into 13 points, 5 assists, and 2 steals. The Huskies also

Before UConn's final regular season game of the 1989–90 season, the university honored Tate George for his dedication to the basketball program.

George beats his man on the baseline as part of a typically well-balanced performance: 13 points, 5 assists, and 2 steals. A nice way to round out his career at Connecticut.

came up with yet another steal and a reverse layup. Then Smith scored the next five points, giving UConn an 11–0 lead in the span of 1:39.

UConn's defense held Seton Hall scoreless until the 13:08 mark in the first half. The Pirates shot just 22.7 percent and trailed 35–24 at the break. UConn shot 53.8 percent in the first half.

The second half began with Henefeld picking up another of his 6 steals and finding Burrell at the other end of the court for the slam. The dunk began another run for the Huskies, this one a 13–4 spurt that sealed the Pirates' fate. UConn now led by 20 with 13:57 to go. The fans could just sit back and enjoy the rest of the game without having to worry about the final out-

Thankfully, Chris Smith will be a Husky for a couple more seasons. Here, Smith concentrates on the hoop while taking an off-balance shot.

got fine production from their bench. Cyrulik, Burrell, Williams, and Gwynn all played at least ten minutes and combined for 20 points. Toraino Walker played nine minutes and scored 3, while Steve Pikiell added a basket as well. Calhoun was fine-tuning his bench for the match-up with Georgetown.

As the final minutes of the Seton Hall game ticked away, the crowd repeatedly chanted, "We want Georgetown." Gampel Pavilion had seen its last game for 1989–90. UConn won all five, four of them Big East games, all of them sellouts. The atmosphere was scintillating.

Coach Calhoun said that at the 1990 Big East postseason meeting, an argument developed. Syracuse coach Boeheim said it was unfair for Syracuse to have to play UConn in Hartford instead of Storrs. Then Seton Hall's P. J. Carlesimo got up and said, "Wait a minute, you haven't played at Gampel."

The Huskies didn't figure to play in front of a home crowd again this season. Their fans thanked them for the season by giving them a rousing ovation as they left the court. What they did not know was the Huskies would be back in Hartford for a pair of NCAA tournament games. That was of small consequence now, however. UConn had a date with Georgetown in Landover, Maryland.

Smith scored a game-high 21 points in this win over the Pirates, including this breakaway.

117

Chapter 16

Meet the (Co-)Champs
February 28, March 3, 1990

With two regular-season games to go, the 1989–90 Huskies already owned the school record for most wins in a season (24). UConn remained a game ahead of Georgetown and Syracuse in the race for the Big East crown. The Huskies also led both in the national polls. UConn was fourth in the AP poll—its highest ranking ever—behind Kansas, Missouri, and UNLV. (Georgetown began the week seventh, while Syracuse was tenth.) In the CNN/*USA Today* poll UConn was fifth, while UPI put UConn at sixth.

While UConn was getting more and more national attention, the local coverage intensified. Connecticut newspapers started sending at least two reporters to each game, and all four major television stations followed the Huskies' every move, doing satellite linkups from Storrs or wherever the team was playing. Bandwagon hopping became addictive in the state.

UConn and a couple of busloads of fans packed up and headed down Interstate 95 to the Capital Centre. The Huskies knew a win would give them a share of the Big East title, but they also knew Georgetown was especially tough at home. UConn had not won in Landover since 1981–82, a year in which the Hoyas finished second in the nation.

Georgetown's starting five was as good as any in the nation. Leading scorer Mark Tillmon averaged 20 points a game while backcourt partner Dwayne Bryant had a 12.4-point average. But the Hoyas' real weapons were up front: 6'10" Alonzo Mourning and 7'2" Dikembe Mutombo. The latter was averaging more than 10 points and 10 rebounds and had over 100 blocked shots. Mourning, another intimidator, was averaging 17 points and 8.4 rebounds. Forward Anthony Allen (2.1 p.p.g.) was the other starter.

Syracuse had treated its rematch with UConn as though it was playing Georgetown, and the Hoyas approached their February 28 showdown with the Huskies with the intensity usually reserved for the Orangemen. For UConn, Smith, Henefeld, George, Sellers, and DePriest would get the nod. A sellout of 19,035 was on hand to witness what figured to be a defensive struggle. UConn was giving up 66 points a game, Georgetown 64.5.

UConn came out strong, taking a 5-point lead 6:40 into the game. But the Hoyas were out to avoid a repeat of January 20 in Hartford. Georgetown forced UConn into taking some bad shots, created some turnovers, and grabbed a 17–13 lead.

The Huskies got 33 shots in the first half but connected on just 8. They were 3 of 14 on three-pointers. The 24.2 percent shooting was a season's low. Mutombo blocked three shots for the Hoyas, and he was unstoppable on offense. The sophomore from Zaire hit short jump shots, hooks, and layups to finish the half with 13 points and 11 rebounds. UConn had lost all four of the previous games in which it trailed at the half and they trailed here, 38–28.

Chris Smith led the Huskies with 7 first-half points, but he seemed to be doing too much. UConn began getting away from the passing and distributing that had made it a 24-4 team.

Early in the second half, Mourning scored in the paint to extend the Hoya lead to 13. The Huskies needed a run now, or the Hoyas figured to waltz to victory.

George hit 2 of his 10 points moments later to cut the margin to 43–32. UConn eventually trimmed its deficit to five, but was unable to capitalize on more Georgetown turnovers. Twenty-five times in the game Georgetown would turn the ball over; however, UConn's running game never got in gear to score off those miscues. The Huskies shot a dismal 11 for 34 in the second half.

Meanwhile, the Hoyas were pulling an inside job on UConn. Mutombo and Mourning continued to knock down high-percentage shots. For the game Mourning hit all five of his shots for 20 points, while Mutombo (5 of 7) scored 15 (Bryant tied Mourning for high scorer). And the duo's defensive presence forced UConn to shoot from the perimeter all night. Smith launched 26 attempts, 12 from three-point range. Overall the Huskies hit on just 6 of 26 three-pointers.

Calhoun became so frustrated that he earned

a technical foul. His team shot 28.4 percent for the game and wound up losing, 84–64.

In New Jersey, Syracuse struggled past Seton Hall, 71–69. Now the Big East championship picture was a whole lot clearer. Syracuse, Georgetown, and UConn all were 11–4 heading into the final games. The Huskies were in the best position; they merely had to defeat 1–14 Boston College for a share of their first Big East championship. Georgetown and Syracuse would square off in the Carrier Dome, Sunday, March 4, for the other share.

No matter what game had been called the "biggest" or "most important" for UConn in the season, this March 3 contest at BC certainly was of the utmost. It meant being Big East champions. The task did not seem all that difficult; the Eagles were 8–18 and had lost 14 of their last 16 games. Still, Calhoun was not wild about making the ninety-minute trip north. "To play Boston College at Boston College is somewhere between hemorrhoids and root canal work. It is a very difficult proposition for us," he said.

The Eagles assuredly did not want to see UConn take the Big East title in their own backyard. The rivalry became downright nasty earlier in the week when a commentary appeared in *The Heights*, Boston College's weekly student newspaper, that blasted the UConn program.

"So they build the beautiful, new, lovely, stunning, ravishing Harry A. Gampel Pavilion down at the University of Connecticut. Not a bad building if you like concrete decor. It's like having a blank check to buy any car you want, and purchasing a Yugo," Mike Damauro wrote. He went on to add, "It's also quite possible that there's nothing else to do down at the Land that God Forgot than to come to the beautiful, new, lovely, stunning, ravishing Harry A. Gampel Pavilion and make a horse's derriere out of yourself." The vindictiveness continued: "Then there's Jim Calhoun. Jim Calhoun, basketball coach, is outstanding. Jim Calhoun, person, is contemptible."

With BC on spring break, many students sold their tickets to UConn fans. The Huskies had been the only team in the nation to play this season on three different home courts (Hartford Civic Center, Field House, and Gampel Pavilion), and now they could unofficially add Conte Forum to that list. More than half of the 8,604 seats were filled with UConn faithful.

Less than three minutes into the game, Lyman DePriest gave the fans their money's worth. He made the first of UConn's 11 steals on the night, then raced the length of the court for a tomahawk jam. Later in the half, Henefeld hit a jumper and then a three-pointer to give UConn a 23-18 lead. Soon after, Gwynn fed Sellers for a slam. UConn was on its way.

The Huskies shot 54.2 percent from the field, hit 21 of 24 free throws, and took a 48-38 lead into the locker room. Twenty minutes separated UConn from a Big East championship.

Maybe it was still too early to celebrate, but the party was starting after back-to-back field goals by Sellers made it a 20-point lead with 5:04 to go. The Huskies glided home for a 95-74 win on the strength of five double-digit scoring performances: Henefeld, 18; Sellers, 16; Smith, 15; Gwynn, 13; and George, 12. UConn made good on a whopping 38 of 44 free throws, and forced 24 BC turnovers. Henefeld's 2 thefts gave him 59 for the Big East season, tying the conference mark held by Michael Adams.

BC's final 1-15 record was the Big East's worst in seven years. Meanwhile, UConn had finished higher than fourth for the first time in league history. Better yet, the Big East's only state school owned the keys to the penthouse.

"It brought tears to my eyes, thinking about how far the program has turned around," George said afterward. "After all the yelling, especially after today. It was a special highlight." On a cold March night the Huskies, who had not finished better than seventh since 1981-82, proved they indeed belonged in the Big East. The greatest regular season in UConn history was over, a record of 25-5 to show for it. The statewide celebration was well under way.

To consider the improbability of what had just happened, one must look back at the history of the Big East. No team had ever finished seven places higher than predicted in the pre-season. And the Huskies' 12-4 record represented the

best one-year improvement in league history; UConn had gone 6-10 in 1988-89.

How did UConn win the Big East title? Sure, good fortune was involved, but it was really teamwork and defense. For the entire 1989-90 regular season, UConn made 396 steals and forced 641 turnovers, way up from 275 and 537, respectively, in 1988-89. Henefeld's 120 steals in the regular season ranked second in the nation. He also was contributing 12 points and 5.9 rebounds a game. Smith led the team in scoring at 16.8 per game. George was averaging 11.1 points and 5 assists and had 57 steals; Sellers had started all 30 games, averaging 9.5 points. Gwynn was still the spark off the bench, and Burrell was also playing well. Cyrulik, DePriest, Williams, Walker, and Steve Pikiell provided the depth. UConn's adaptation to Calhoun's method of teaching defense was the ultimate factor in the team's success.

The title would be a shared one, but it also meant that either Georgetown or Syracuse would finish lower than UConn in the final standings. That alone would bring a smile to any UConn fan. Once it all had sunk in and the cleanup from the celebrations and the night of merriment was completed, the newly crowned Big East champion Huskies and their fans tuned into the Georgetown-Syracuse game the next day.

The host Orangemen were looking to complete a sweep of the Hoyas and send seniors Derrick Coleman and Stephen Thompson out with their second Big East regular-season title.

Georgetown built an early 10-point lead, but Syracuse fought back to make it 36-33. Then Hoyas coach John Thompson, protesting a foul call, was slapped with a technical foul by each of the three referees at the same time. Thompson was also ejected, much to the delight of the record 33,015 on hand. Coleman, who had been fouled, sank 7 of 8 free throws, and then Billy Owens hit a three. Thompson added a jam to give Syracuse a 45-40 lead at halftime.

Georgetown would come back and eventually regain the lead, 79-78, late in regulation. With four seconds left, Mourning hit two free throws to put Georgetown up 81-79. UConn and Georgetown seemed destined for a coin flip that would determine the Big East tournament's top seed. But Syracuse, with some resuscitation from the Hoyas' Sam Jefferson, still had a pulse. Jefferson fouled Owens as he made a desperation drive down the court. Owens hit both free throws to send the game into overtime. Then Thompson hit the game-winning shot with 25 seconds left in overtime. Syracuse came away with an 89–87 victory and a share of the Big East title. The Orangemen's two wins over the Hoyas gave them the number-one seed for the Big East tournament in New York. Syracuse would face the winner of the March 8, Pittsburgh–Boston College game, while UConn would meet Seton Hall.

The regular season had been special, but the season was by no means over for the Huskies. The next few weeks would mean the difference between a team that would be remembered for a few years to come, and one that would be the standard by which future UConn teams would be measured. A new season was about to begin, as was another chapter in the history of UConn basketball.

Chapter 17

UConn's Garden Party
March 9, 10, 11, 1990

The Huskies had five days to prepare for their match-up with Seton Hall. The week began with UConn falling to eighth in the AP poll. The UPI and CNN/*USA Today* polls had the Huskies seventh and sixth, respectively. Oklahoma topped the AP poll, followed by Kansas, UNLV, Syracuse, Georgetown, Missouri, and Michigan State. By this point in the season, the polls were of small consequence. The tournaments would determine the true number ones.

Also at week's start, the Big East handed out the hardware. To the surprise of absolutely no one, Henefeld was voted rookie of the year. He was also named to the all-rookie team, and third-team all-conference. Smith, the league's seventh-leading scorer (he also had 110 assists and 51 steals on the season) made the second team. George joined Henefeld on the third team while Burrell accompanied Henefeld on the all-rookie team. Despite the injury to his knee, Burrell started more than half of UConn's regular-season games and averaged 8.2 points and 5.2 rebounds with 46 steals.

There was no award for UConn's bench, which was contributing more than 26 points per game. But honors didn't really mean much to a first-place team that didn't have a first-team all-conference selection. The way Calhoun had set up his system, no particular player was going to be the star. UConn was out to prove that a team did not need a Derrick Coleman or an Alonzo Mourning to win the conference tournament.

The "steal curtain" was the name of UConn's premier player. The Huskies were averaging 13.2 steals a game, and four players ranked among the top twelve on the school's all-time single-season list after the regular year: Henefeld (1), George (4), Smith (8), and Burrell (12). Success in the Big East tournament, and thereafter, would come from this defense.

The Huskies spent part of their relaxation time watching the UConn women battle Providence for the Big East tournament championship at Gampel Pavilion. It was the women's day in the sun (even though they lost, 82–61), but it was the men's team which received much of the attention. Whenever they left their seats, they were swarmed by children for autographs. At the season's outset, none of these kids knew who Henefeld, or any of his teammates, was.

The Huskies began their spring break a couple days early as they departed for New York on Wednesday. The Big East tournament had been an exclusive engagement won by only three teams in its first ten years. Georgetown owned six titles, including four of the previous six. Syracuse took the title in 1988 and in 1981, when it was held in the Carrier Dome. After 1982, when the tournament was played in Hartford, the Big East extravaganza was shifted to Madison Square Garden. St. John's Redmen were hometown heroes when they captured the championship in 1983 and 1986. Villanova and Boston College were the only other teams to have reached the championship game.

UConn had advanced to the semifinals just

Rod Sellers is helped off the court after injuring his knee early in the game against the Georgetown Hoyas. Sellers sat out the rest of the game.
(Photo by Michael T. Kiernan/*New Haven Register*)

once, in the inaugural year of 1980. For the next seven tournaments, UConn was not able to get through its first game. In 1988, the ninth-seeded Huskies downed Providence in the eight-nine game, but then they lost in the quarterfinals to Pitt.

UConn came into the 1989 tournament with sixteen regular-season victories. A defeat of second-seeded Seton Hall might have landed the Huskies in the NCAA tournament, but UConn dropped the game, 74–66. Seton Hall went on to become the national runner-up, while UConn went back to the NIT. However, the teams had traded places in 1990. UConn was the second seed and Seton Hall the seventh.

On Thursday, the day prior to the quarterfinals, the Big East announced its 1990 coach of the year. There was no real suspense involved—the honor would have to go to Jim Calhoun.

His speech mannerisms and quick answers to questions force one to listen closely. He may sound nervous, but he's not. The virtually bare walls of his office and nearly empty shelves on his bookcase may make one think he's boring. But he isn't. The way he interrupts an interview to answer the phone might make him seem indifferent. But he never is.

"One of the main reasons we hired Jim Calhoun four years ago is because we felt this was not a job for someone to cut their teeth on as a new coach," says Tim Tolokan, sports information director at the university. "The Connecticut job is too tough. P.R.-wise it's too tough. Coaching-wise it's too tough. And when we brought him in four years ago we knew one thing—that he had been a head coach at a Division I program for fourteen years. You can't buy that experience."

Neither did Jim Calhoun.

Calhoun's ties to New England and basketball are obvious if you simply plot the course of his history. He grew up in Braintree, Massachusetts, playing basketball, football, and baseball. He moved across the state to Springfield for his college years and excelled as a Little All-American while serving as captain of the basketball squad his senior year at American International College. Then he became an assistant coach at his alma mater for two years, before

(Photo by Michael T. Kiernan/*New Haven Register*)

Toraino Walker (42) and Murray Williams battle Alonzo Mourning (33) for a loose ball. Along with Dan Cyrulik, Walker filled in admirably for the injured Sellers.

Tate George beats Mourning to the hoop and lays in a finger roll.

coming to Connecticut for the first time to coach at Old Lyme High School.

Other jobs followed. After one year at Westport High School in New Bedford, Massachusetts, Calhoun moved on to Dedham High School in Dedham, Massachusetts, where he quickly rebuilt the program. He took his last high school team to the State Division I semifinals in 1971–72. From there came the chance that few coaches get—to become a college head coach. For Calhoun it was in the comfy confines of his old stomping grounds, Boston, at Northeastern University.

While at Northeastern, Calhoun had the misfortune of being the head coach at a time when the program was moving up to Division I. Calhoun and others close to the team had their doubts.

"Jim elevated us kicking and screaming every inch of the way," remembers Jack Grinold, the director of sports information at Northeastern. "But Jim comprises the best of Boston, the affability of the Irish and the work ethic of the Puritan, and uses it to his advantage."

His ability to recruit players who fit his program has helped set Calhoun above the rest. Whether it be keeping Chris Smith in his home state or flying to Israel to bring Nadav Henefeld to a foreign land, it his work ethic that makes it all possible. Once during a late Friday evening in June 1978, Calhoun was working at his Northeastern desk when the phone rang. On the other end was a young man from Pittsburgh named Peter Harris.

"I'll bet that if you went around the country at approximately 6 o'clock that Friday evening in June," Grinold said, "Jim might have been the only one of the 260-odd college basketball coaches in his office. It was with that phone call and the recruitment of Peter Harris that our program turned around."

That same kind of diligence had helped turn this year into the Dream Season. "As Dee Rowe said, Jim did a helluva job coaching, that goes without saying," said Tolokan. "But Jim also did a helluva job motivating, and he pushed the buttons at the right time. It was uncanny."

Perhaps, but the precedent was set years ago at Northeastern. Turning around wayward programs is in Calhoun's blood. About UConn's

The UConn bench reacts to the action on the court. The Huskies defeated the Hoyas for the second time that year, 65–60.

success, Grinold said, "It doesn't surprise us. We saw him do the same thing here. We knew the mechanisms were in place down there with the league and the commitment to the sport."

In his first year at Northeastern, Calhoun was runner-up to Dave Gavitt of Providence as New England coach of the year. For 1989–90, Calhoun received national coach-of-the-year honors from AP, UPI, CBS-TV Sports, *Basketball Weekly,* and *The Sporting News.*

As the media descended upon Calhoun following the announcement of his awards, the other coaches entered for the pre-tournament press conference. Unlike the preseason gathering, Calhoun was one of the more sought-after coaches. No longer did he have to defend the abilities of his team; thirty games had already done that. Now Calhoun had to explain how his team was going to win the Big East tournament championship.

Shortly before the Seton Hall game, it was announced that UConn President John Casteen III was leaving to become president of the University of Virginia. Casteen had served as Virginia's secretary of education prior to his five years at UConn, and had been vocal about the lack of state funding for the university. A budget deficit had forced state lawmakers to cut the university's budget, leading to protests by Casteen and the student body. On campus, there were also complaints of racial harassment, overcrowded classes, and the problems facing the school of engineering.

Todd Turner, UConn's athletic director, would later announce that he was leaving as well. It was not the best of times, but the UConn basketball team gave the school something it could be proud about. The Huskies had helped mend a university that was splitting at the seams.

Calhoun's troops came out for Seton Hall with their press running on all cylinders. Burrell started the game to provide more quickness and agility. In the first half, UConn dismantled the Pirates' attack, limiting them to 40.9 percent shooting from the floor. Though the Huskies hit just 37.9 percent of their shots, they led, 36–26, at the half.

The backcourt duo of Smith and George were keeping the Huskies on top. The two combined

(Photo by Michael T. Kiernan/*New Haven Register*)

Syracuse guard Michael Edwards sets up for a three-pointer in front of UConn's expectant coaching staff.

for 36 points in the game, and did the job on the defensive end as well. In the second half the Huskies began to force turnover after turnover, and collect steal after steal. It was a microcosm of the season. UConn would score, put on the full-court press and force either a turnover or a steal, and score again. As the game wound down, it became clear to the UConn fans in attendance and everywhere else that the Huskies were going to the semifinals for the first time in ten years.

The numbers explained how UConn recorded the 76–58 win over Seton Hall. UConn forced 24 turnovers and limited the Pirates to 33.3 percent shooting in the second half (36.5 percent overall). And the Huskies made a tournament-record 17 steals—6 by George and 5 by Henefeld. George also scored a team-high 20 points on 7 of 9 shooting from the floor. Smith, though having his problems from the field, hit all 8 of his foul shots and finished with 16 points.

As the Huskies left the Garden that Friday afternoon, they knew their next opponent would be Georgetown. In the second game of the afternoon, the Hoyas had downed Providence in a tight contest. The teams' third meeting of the year would begin in less than twenty-four hours. In the second semifinal, Villanova would meet top-seeded Syracuse.

The Huskies walked onto the court Saturday with a quiet confidence, as if to say that nothing was going to derail them. For Georgetown, though, playing in the Big East semifinals was nothing new. The Hoyas were out to prove their 20-point victory over UConn meant more than their January 20 loss to the Huskies.

The game would be nationally televised by CBS. This, of course, was nothing new for Georgetown. But UConn? The Huskies had not been on network television since the seventies, when they still were a member of the Eastern College Athletic Conference and NBC covered the league's games.

Georgetown looked to come out strong and attack, and the Huskies knew they would have to use everything in their arsenal to win this one. But just two minutes into the game, the Huskies lost one of their most potent weapons when center Rod Sellers went down with a knee injury. As Sellers sat on the court, holding onto his injured leg, Connecticut fans might have felt a noose tightening around their necks. As the first half ended, UConn fans had reason to worry. Georgetown had hit 59.1 percent of its first-half shots as it led, 36-30, at the break.

The 6-point lead did not seem insurmountable, but UConn had not come back to win a game after trailing at the half the entire season. But nobody was ready to give up. If the Huskies just stuck with Calhoun's system and did what they had all year long, they could alter their fate. But Georgetown was determined to hold onto its lead, and after Mark Tillmon (23 points) hit a three-pointer, Georgetown led by eight nearing the midway part of the second half. UConn, despite being down, found a positive in that Dikembe Mutombo, who had been Georgetown's major weapon late in the season, was

being held virtually scoreless and soon would be on the bench with foul trouble.

Then the Huskies got the run they needed. They outscored Georgetown, 14-0, over an eight-minute span. Gwynn started the charge with a three-pointer, but once again UConn relied on its defense to make the difference. The Hoyas were trapped into 19 turnovers on the day, as UConn had 10 steals by seven different players. As UConn took the lead, the cheers from the Connecticut fans began to rise like a chorus.

The Georgetown bench sensed the game slipping away. Big men Alonzo Mourning and Mutombo were held to just 12 and 4 points, respectively. They were contained by the unlikely pair of Toraino Walker and Dan Cyrulik, who shared time in the middle after Sellers went down. The two combined for just 10 points, but they hit the boards hard and prevented Georgetown's big men from doing significant damage down low.

Chris Smith is one of the first Huskies to climb up and cut down the net after UConn beat Syracuse, 78-75, for the Big East Championship.
(Photo by Michael Kiernan/*New Haven Register*)

The minutes that Calhoun had given Walker throughout the year certainly aided the freshman in this spot.

The final was UConn 65, Georgetown 60. The Husky fans stood in disbelief. Their heroes had defeated the big, bad Hoyas for the second time this season, another first for the program.

Afterward, UConn watched Syracuse get by Villanova in the second semifinal, 73–61. Not only was Syracuse the tournament's number one seed, but the Orange entered the title game with a six-game winning streak—all Big East games. They also had defeated all seven of the Top 20 teams they had faced to date.

Cyrulik got the nod at center for the injured Sellers. In the two earlier games against Syracuse, Sellers had scored just 10 points. But in the Huskies' victory, he had 8 points and 8 rebounds. The Huskies figured to miss his presence underneath the basket. The lanky 6'9" sophomore would set the picks, he could take the charge and shoot the jumper when needed. It would now be

John Gwynn takes his turn snipping down the net.
(Photo by Michael T. Kiernan/New Haven Register)

up to the 7'1" Cyrulik and the 6'6" Walker to fill the void.

The Huskies knew if they won they might be going to Hartford for the opening rounds of the NCAA tournament. But travel arrangements were far from their minds, especially after Syracuse ran out to a 10–0 lead. The Huskies were probably a bit nervous, and Calhoun called a timeout to quell the jitters.

Smith finally got UConn on the scoreboard by drilling a jumper. Meanwhile, Syracuse had come out of the time-out lackadaisically. Perhaps the Orange figured they had UConn down and out. Syracuse proceeded to turn the ball over nine times in one stretch, and the Huskies came storming back. The defense created the chances, and the offense capitalized. When Walker hit on a short jumper UConn had their tie, 29–29.

Syracuse outshot UConn 53.8 to 48.5 percent in the first half, but trailed 42–35 at the intermission. The screaming chorus known as the UConn student section was singing a masterpiece. Connecticut, the newcomer, was showing Syracuse, the bully on the Big East block, a few things.

CBS play-by-play man Brent Musburger slipped during the broadcast when he referred to Syracuse as the Big East regular-season champion. However, co-champ Connecticut was making a statement to the nation on this Sunday afternoon. Guards Chris Smith and Tate George, along with John Gwynn off the bench, were the keys to this game. Syracuse coach Jim Boeheim would later say Connecticut's guards were "too much for us."

A pair of free throws by Coleman pulled the Orangemen within two points in the second half. But UConn stood tough in this duel of wills. Gwynn came right back and canned an 18-foot jump shot for a 55–51 UConn lead. Syracuse's Stevie Thompson eventually tied the score at 57. Then Gwynn answered with a three-pointer to put UConn up, 60–57.

The game continued to stay tight, and with 8 seconds to go UConn held a 76–72 lead. George stepped to the line for a pressure-packed one-and-bonus. The first shot went up and in. George pumped his fist in the air. He was staring right into the UConn student section, and they certainly were not trying to distract him as they raised their hands above their heads for George's second attempt. It too was good.

UConn led by six as Syracuse rushed the ball up court. Tony Scott hit a three-point buzzer beater, but it wasn't enough. The Huskies had taken the Big East championship, 78–75. The 200-plus UConn students at courtside rushed the floor. The P.A. announcer asked everyone to stay off the court, but there was no holding them back. Security personnel stood in their way, and they too could not stop the celebration. There had been no stopping the Huskies, and now there was no stopping their fans.

The fans stayed on the court, along with the pep band, cheerleaders, and Husky dog mascot, as the Huskies cut down the nets. Calhoun had gone a few rows into the crowd to hug his wife, Pat. This was a moment a coach dreams of, and Calhoun watched his players share in it, Gwynn especially. During the game the intense Gwynn repeatedly pumped his fists into the air. Now, as he took his cut at the net, he flashed a coast-to-coast grin that was so big it made any UConn fan smile. It was the realization of a dream that made others cry.

How did UConn win this game? Defense, of course, was an integral part. Syracuse did hit on 56.9 percent of its shots, but the Huskies forced 20 turnovers and made 13 steals. UConn also had four double-figure scorers: George with 22; Smith, 20; Gwynn, 16 (in twelve minutes of play); and Walker, 11. Defensively, Walker, Cyrulik, Henefeld, and Burrell helped hold Syracuse's front line of Derrick Coleman, Billy Owens, and LeRon Ellis to a total of 28 points.

Co-captains George and Steve Pikiell accepted the championship trophy from Associate Commissioner Mike Tranghese. Just two years earlier they were members of the last-place team in the Big East, and now they were on top. The honors for UConn did not end there. George and Gwynn were named to the all-tournament team, as was Chris Smith.

Smith received the David Gavitt Award as the Most Valuable Player. It was Smith's tournament in almost every sense. Connecticut's guards led the way, and Smith was their leader. He scored 54 points for the tournament.

His hometown is Bridgeport, Connecticut, and he's a starting guard for the University of Connecticut basketball team. Seem odd? It might if it were years past and the Smith in question was named Charles. But this was Chris Smith, the Huskies' leading scorer in 1989–90. "Smitty" knew long ago he wanted to attend UConn. He felt it important for Connecticut kids to play for their state university.

Smith started every game the Huskies played in 1989–90 and averaged a team-leading 17.2 points a game. Two years ago he had become the third straight Connecticut prep player of the year to shun the other Big East powers and stay in his home state. While this may not seem too unusual, it was hardly a given that the state's best player would attend UConn.

Charles Smith, a friend of Smitty's and another Bridgeport native, left the confines of the Nutmeg State for the University of Pittsburgh in 1984. While the Los Angeles Clipper can still be found on the playgrounds of Bridgeport playing pick-up games with friends, he never donned a Connecticut jersey.

Chris Smith, though, has done just fine in Calhoun's system. A hard worker and tremendous athlete, he averaged a whopping 35 minutes in Big East contests. Some observers saw Smitty for the true contribution he made to the success of the Dream Season. Said Gil Santos of the Big East Network, "He is another prime example of the unselfish team the Huskies were. He can create a shot, he can shoot off the dribble, and he has great range. He could have been one of the top three scorers in the league."

One net had come down and there was another to go. Toraino Walker lofted Calhoun up on his shoulders and the coach proceeded to clip. The smile on his face told the story.

The celebrations would finally end, and less than an hour after the game the NCAA tournament selection committee would announce its sixty-four-team field. By winning the Big East tournament UConn received the conference's automatic bid and was virtually guaranteed a number one seed in one of the four regions. The dance was about to begin, and for the first time in eleven years UConn had an invitation.

Chapter 18

Hartford Is Where the Home Is

March 15, 17, 1990

The Big East championship was the greatest trophy ever captured in the ninety years of UConn basketball. But there was still another elusive prize out there. Where would this Cinderella team, by no means an underdog anymore, begin its quest for college basketball's top honor? It did not take the Huskies long to find out.

Shortly after the nets were brought down in Madison Square Garden, the Huskies sat down to see where their next step would take them. UConn was the last Big East team since the inception of the conference to make the NCAAs. The first team that came up on the board for the East Regional was Connecticut, and it would be playing its first two rounds at the Hartford Civic Center. According to the NCAA, a team's home court is where it plays more than half its home games. In that regard, UConn had no "official" home court in 1989-90. UConn played five of its eighteen "home" games at the Field House, five more in Gampel Pavilion, and the other eight at Hartford.

Was the decision fair? Many said it wasn't.

However, UConn was hosting the first- and second-round games in Hartford, and if the Huskies were sent instead to Atlanta they would have to play on Friday and Sunday. This meant that Tim Tolokan, UConn's sports information director, would have had to travel back and forth between Atlanta and Hartford. Regardless of the details, UConn was home for rounds one and two.

As a top seed, UConn could practically count on advancing to the second round. Since the 1985 inception of the sixty-four-team field, with four brackets of sixteen teams, no number one seed had lost in the first round. Boston University (18-11), with its automatic bid from the North Atlantic Conference, would be the Huskies' first-round opponent on Thursday. The winner would play either eighth-seeded Indiana (18-10) or number nine California (21-9). The other side of the Hartford bracket had Clemson against Brigham Young and LaSalle versus Southern Mississippi.

In the final AP poll released on the Monday after the Big East tournament, Oklahoma,

UNLV, and Connecticut comprised the top three. This was the highest ranking ever for a UConn team, but the NCAA tournament had arrived and the polls didn't mean a thing.

Six teams from the Big East made the field: UConn, Syracuse, Georgetown, St. John's, Villanova, and Providence.

There was a twist to the BU-UConn matchup. BU coach Mike Jarvis and UConn's Calhoun had not been the best of friends over the years. The dispute began when Calhoun was at Northeastern, and ever since it had made for an interesting footnote to their meetings. The Huskies would have the 15,937 fans in their favor, and they had the better team. The question was how long would it take UConn to eliminate BU. In the afternoon session that March 15, Clemson rallied in the final seconds to defeat BYU, 49-47. LaSalle improved to 30-1 with a 79-63 victory over Southern Mississippi in the second game.

The second session would be highlighted by UConn's first NCAA tournament game in eleven years. With a healthy Rod Sellers returning, Calhoun went with the same lineup that he opened the Big East tournament with. This was UConn's first game in Hartford since the stirring January 20 upset of Georgetown and the Huskies seemed happy to be back. They raced out to a 10-0 lead just 3:41 into the game.

Senior center Rod Moses helped get the Terriers back in the game with 8 first-half points, and BU outscored UConn, 28-19, for the remainder of the half. Suddenly, the home court didn't seem that great an advantage.

The Huskies were still leading, though, and as they came out for the second half the fans rose to their feet and began their ritual clapping. The Huskies answered that call immediately; Smith canned a three-pointer to make it 32-28. The bucket gave the Huskies some room to work with, but BU was not ready to pack it in just yet.

Steven Key's three-pointer put BU up, 33-32, at 18:49. And when the Terriers extended their lead to 41-38, Calhoun took a much-needed time-out.

Smith tied the score at 41 when he hit on one of his four three-pointers. Then Henefeld stepped into the spotlight. He scored on a rare jam and then netted UConn's next six points.

Turnovers continually haunted the Terriers, 27 in all, and UConn's defense held them without a field goal for a 6:48 span. In that time, the Huskies went on a 21-1 run that gave them a 59-44 lead.

UConn would outscore the Terriers, 47-24, in the second half and walk away with a 76-52 victory. Henefeld and Smith each scored 19 while Gwynn added 10 off the bench. And the "steal curtain" produced a tournament-record 19 steals. Afterward, Jarvis said, "We ran out of gas. The next team that they face will come in with a lot more gas, so UConn should fill up."

The Huskies retreated to a nearby hotel, where they relaxed and watched the Indiana-California game. Hoosier coach Bob Knight was not particularly fond of Hartford. In 1988, the year after winning the NCAA championship, the Hoosiers came into Hartford and subsequently lost to Richmond in the first round.

The same scenario prevailed in 1990. With the score tied at 63, the Hoosiers fouled California guard Keith Smith with three seconds left. He hit both free throws, and Indiana missed a desperation shot to give California the 65-63 victory.

The matchups for Saturday in Hartford were set. UConn would play California in the opening game, followed by LaSalle versus Clemson. The Huskies had the experience of an NCAA game behind them, not to mention 16,011 fans, and now they sought victory number 30, an unthinkable achievement back in November.

The sellout crowd had the St. Patrick's day spirit as it looked to send the Huskies on to the regional semifinals in East Rutherford, New Jersey. Almost one year ago to the day, on the same floor, UConn had edged the Golden Bears, 73-72, in an NIT second-round game.

That was then, this was now. In the first five minutes UConn used defense, precision passing, and some slam dunks to open up a 17-2 lead. In that span, California turned the ball over eight times. The roof was falling in on the Bears and it wasn't only from the noise UConn fans were making. By halftime, the Huskies' cushion was 42-26.

UConn shot just 32.3 percent in the second half, but once again defense was the key. UConn forced California into 28 turnovers and made 16 steals. The Huskies had 471 steals overall and were approaching Oklahoma's NCAA record of 486 in 1987–88. California was rudely excused from the tournament by a 74–54 count.

Smith led the way with 24 points. Burrell scored 13 while Henefeld and George added 10 each. The only downer was Sellers leaving the game in the second half when his injured knee flared up again. At this point, though, Sellers and his teammates would walk to the Meadowlands if they had to.

UConn's regional semifinal opponent would be Clemson, which rallied past LaSalle, 79–75, in the second game at Hartford. Duke, a 76–72 victor over St. John's, and UCLA would meet in the other semi.

Upsets and close games abounded in this tournament. Just three teams, UConn, UNLV, and Loyola–Marymount, had won each of their first two games by more than ten points. The first two games may have seemed a bit too easy for the Huskies, but game three against Clemson's comeback kids figured to be plenty challenging.

Chapter 19

Miracle in the Meadowlands
March 22, 24, 1990

The UConn student body was back from spring break and ready to make some noise. The NIT championship in 1988 had brought UConn together in a common celebration, but this run for the national championship was even better. The fans wanted more, and they would get it in UConn's regional semifinal match with Clemson.

The 26–8 Tigers, regular-season champions of the ACC for the first time ever, had advanced to the round of sixteen for just the second time in seventy-nine years. Clemson coach Cliff Ellis exemplified the way his team had risen from the shadows of the football program. He took over the Tigers in 1985–86, after they had finished 3–11 in the ACC. Ellis came from South Alabama, where he turned the program around and left with a record of 171–84.

Taking the Clemson job was a huge challenge for Ellis, who still had to overcome the belief that Clemson was basically a football school. He also had the difficulty of having to recruit against such traditional powerhouses as Duke and North Carolina. Ellis' answer was to recruit nationally, not just regionally. His center, 6'11" Elden Campbell, was from Inglewood, California. Another 6'11" player, Dale Davis, came from Toccoa, Georgia.

Another big man almost went to Clemson. UConn sophomore Rod Sellers, from Florence, South Carolina, almost chose Clemson, too. "We recruited Sellers. Rod is a great human being and he came from a great program," Ellis said. "But we did not have a tremendous need for him with Campbell and Davis. So we encouraged him to go to the University of Connecticut." To which Calhoun would respond, "I would like to publicly thank Cliff Ellis for telling that to Rod."

Campbell and Davis, Clemson's "Duo of Doom," were in top form this season. Campbell was averaging 16.8 points while Davis was shooting 63 percent for a scoring average of 15.4. But the Tigers could also play some defense.

As, of course, could the Huskies, who had forced 55 turnovers in their first two tournament games. Said Ellis, "They have to put teams away early. We have to watch out for them early in the game."

Clemson was prone to turnovers, having made 502 in 34 games. The Tigers had also been picked for 452 steals. These numbers played right into the Huskies' quick hands.

It was 7:40 p.m. at Brendan Byrne Arena and time to play ball. UConn's fans were directly behind its bench. The Huskies wore their home whites for the third consecutive game. In the home whites UConn had lost just twice all season.

At UConn, nearly 1,200 fans watched the game on a big-screen television at Gampel Pavilion. Thursday night at UConn was the night for merriment, since many students went home on Friday for the weekend. On this particular Thursday night, UConn fans would hardly be able to believe the events to come.

Toraino Walker got the start in place of the injured Sellers. The 6'6" freshman responded instantly with a jumper for a 2-0 lead. UConn kept building on the lead, with Smith and George once again leading the way. UConn held an 11-point lead on two occasions in the first half, and led, 38-29, at the break.

The Huskies' press had forced 16 turnovers thus far, and had stolen the ball 7 times. Things were going UConn's way. The Connecticut students held up signs saying "Duo of Whom." It appeared UConn was on its way to the Final Eight for the first time since 1964. But the Tigers had made too many comebacks in recent games for UConn to take them lightly.

In the second half UConn went right back to work. Smith hit a three to give UConn a 43-29 lead 1:20 into the half. The Huskies would extend the margin to 19, even though they didn't get a single steal in the second half. But this one was still far from over.

Davis and Campbell began to assert themselves down low. The Clemson fans came to life as the huge lead fell to single digits. The Huskies seemed spent, unwilling to answer the challenge by Clemson. The Tigers were beating UConn at its own game—the press. Said Calhoun, "We looked like a freshman team at the end."

UConn turned the ball over nine times down

(Photo by Michael T. Kiernan/*New Haven Register*)

Nadav Henefeld and Chris Smith trap Clemson guard Marion Cash.

the stretch as Clemson closed the gap to 69-67. Davis then wrestled away an offensive rebound, but he stepped out of bounds, giving the ball to the Huskies with just over twenty-one seconds left.

The Pavilion crowd was jumping, sensing the game was finally in hand. The Connecticut fans in the Meadowlands also exhaled. All the Huskies had to do was get the ball inbounds. That task belonged to Henefeld, who was having probably his worst game of the season (2 points, 0 steals).

Henefeld passed the ball in and it was deflected out of bounds. The referees first awarded the ball to UConn, but quickly changed their call. UConn had given it away yet again, and now Clemson had a chance to tie or go ahead. Ellis inserted David Young to launch a long-range shot; Young took the inbounds pass and buried a three. Clemson led for the first time since six minutes into the game, 70-69. As the shot went through, Calhoun removed his jacket. Connecticut's season was ever so close to Judgment Day.

There were shocked fans at Gampel Pavilion, the Meadowlands, and all across the state. What possibly had gone wrong? This was no way for the Big East champion, that prides itself on defense, to go out of the NCAA tournament. But Connecticut fans realized there was still 11.3 seconds left, plenty of time to take a shot.

Tate George dribbled the ball up court and put up a 15-footer. The ball bounced harmlessly off the rim, and Sean Tyson grabbed the rebound with 1.6 seconds left. Burrell immediately fouled him. There were tears, and silence, in the UConn fans' section. George, who was playing just a few miles from his Newark home, said, "After I missed that shot, I just wanted another chance."

The other four Tigers stood near the Clemson bench as Tyson stepped to the line. His shot missed, and the Huskies grabbed the rebound and immediately called time-out. There was but one full second left on the clock.

There was silence at the Pavilion, and in the

Tim Pikiell prays for a miracle as UConn trails, 70–69, with just one second left in the game.
(Photo by Michael T. Kiernan/New Haven Register)

UConn section at the Meadowlands. From the Duke and Clemson fans, the chant of "A-C-C, A-C-C" rang out like a chorus. Burrell took the ball at the baseline after a time-out, and then the Tigers called another one. When the final time-out was over, there was not a single UConn fan sitting down, though the idea of going the length of the court for a basket in one second seemed improbable at best.

During the break, Calhoun told his players they still had a chance. George said, "Coach was yelling, 'It's not over, it's not over.' I told Scott [Burrell] during the time-out that Tyson was not going to foul me."

Burrell would take the ball out. This was usually Henefeld's role, but not so here. Calhoun needed the pitching arm of Burrell. The chants of the ACC fans still could be heard, while the Connecticut fans watched silently. Most of the nation was receiving this game, and according to UConn's Tolokan, the game was drawing a 66 share in Connecticut. That meant two-thirds of the television sets in the state were tuned in.

Burrell took the ball from the referee. The clock would not start until the ball was touched in bounds. Burrell stared at the Clemson press that had limited UConn to 10 points in the previous 12:35. He cocked his arm and fired in the direction of Tate George who was stationed near the opposite baseline. Clemson did not want to foul, and thus the 6'5" George was able to go up and make the catch. "I could hear [UConn assistant coaches] Howie Dickenman and Glen Miller screaming, "Shoot the ball, shoot the ball," George said later. George spun to his left and released the ball from about fourteen feet. Tyson backed away to avoid the foul.

"When it left my hand I lost sight of the ball," George said. "But I heard the crowd roar and I saw the people charge the floor, so I knew it must have gone in," George said. Indeed it had. The "Miracle in the Meadowlands" had been performed. After the shot, Calhoun danced high into the air, the same way Digger Phelps had when Notre Dame defeated Syracuse earlier in the season. But Calhoun would stop to give Cliff Ellis a consoling look and handshake.

UConns fans go wild after Tate George's last second shot had beaten Clemson, 71–70. The Huskies advanced to the Final Eight.

The UConn mascot led the on-court celebration. The Huskies had won their thirty-first game on a one-in-a-million shot. Ellis said after the contest, "This was a typical comeback for our basketball team. We have certainly tasted the thrill of victory, and now we have tasted the agony of defeat."

Back at UConn the party to top all parties was just beginning. More than 4,000 students flooded the area near the North Campus dorms. There they built a bonfire. The UConn police stood by; they, too, were having too much fun to stop the students. The head of the UConn police department, Major Donn Herindeen, said, "We have no complaints about the students . . . we allowed them to vent their energy." For one night, at least, the campus was unified. UConn could thank Tate George.

As a senior at Union Catholic High School in Scotch Plains, New Jersey, Tate George was the captain and most valuable player in 1985. The 6'5" guard was considered among the top 100 recruits in the nation and top 25 in the East. He averaged 21 points, 8 rebounds, 8 assists, and 3 steals a game. That was good enough for Dom Perno to recruit him.

In four years at UConn, George set career marks for games played (128), games started (116), assists (677), and steals (201). But he was more than just a numbers' cruncher—he was a leader.

In the Huskies' win over Syracuse for the Big East tournament title, George scored a game-high 22 points while again showcasing his leadership qualities. Earlier in the year Gil Santos of the Big East Network said of George, "He was the difference. He was the only player on either side who knew how to control the ball and the pace of the game. Even though he made some big shots, it was his general control that stood out. You could see his senior leadership calming people down at crunch time and doing all the things a smart, intelligent player should do."

George endured three years of ups and downs to find the true value of the Dream Season. In a sense, the "marriage" between George, Calhoun, and the Connecticut faithful transcended the good times, bad times, sickness, and health. Now they would part, but George's storybook saga would not end with a handshake and a diploma on a cloudy day in May. On June 27, the New Jersey Nets drafted George as the twenty-second pick on the first round.

Erica George's intuition was right on during Tate's formative years in Newark. The future Husky's mother would not let her young son

146

(Photo by Michael T. Kiernan/*New Haven Register*)

George receives a congratulatory embrace from teammate Smith, who led all scorers with 23 points.

cross the river to see the Knicks play at Madison Square Garden. Instead, she insisted that if he wanted to watch an NBA team, it would be the Nets at the nearby Meadowlands. It is fitting that the apex of George's career to date, the buzzer beater against Clemson in the East Regional semifinals, occurred on the same floor where he envisioned his own boyhood dreams. Now he will play out those dreams for real. When Nets coach Bill Fitch made his congratulatory call to George the night of the draft, his only request was for George to bring some of that luck back to the Meadowlands.

After George's miraculous shot, what could Duke and UCLA do for an encore? They didn't take the court until shortly after 10 p.m., and the contest wasn't over until after midnight. But there was nothing unusual about the end result: Duke advanced to the Final Eight for the fourth time in five years—each time at the Meadowlands—with a 90–81 victory.

Both UConn and Duke entered their Friday press conferences a bit tired. Smith tried to hold his eyes open throughout the interviews, while Burrell and George relived their magic. Calhoun made a reference to the 1984 tournament, when he brought Northeastern to the round of sixteen at the Meadowlands. His Huskies lost that game to Virginia Commonwealth, 70–69, on a last-second jump shot.

Many of the sports writers at the press conference called George's shot the most exciting in college basketball history. There was little doubting that, for sheer excitement and importance alone. While Calhoun and UConn continued to relive the Clemson game, Duke and its coach, Mike Krzyzewski, were talking about making yet another trip to the Final Four. When the subject was broached, the talk of their being there seven times without a national title also came up.

Later that night, four more teams would advance. On Thursday, Texas and Arkansas had moved on to the Midwest final. In the Southeast, Georgia Tech got by Michigan State while Minnesota eliminated Syracuse. That left UConn to carry the banner for the Big East. Advancing in the West were UNLV and Loyola–Marymount.

For UConn, its objective was to stifle the Blue Devils' double-digit scorers: Phil Henderson (17.7 p.p.g.), Christian Laettner (15.8), Alaa Abdelnaby (14.6), and Robert Brickey (12.3). The 27–8 Blue Devils were averaging over 90 points a game while allowing just 75.4. While UConn's defense

George is in good spirits as he limbers up for the East Regional Final against Duke University's Blue Devils.

(Photo by Michael T. Kiernan/*New Haven Register*)

featured the zone press, Duke played a tight and aggressive man-to-man defense.

But Krzyzewski had his own worries, "They play like crazy," he said of the Huskies. "Their press is good and they have good athletes."

UConn and Duke had met twice in the past. In 1964, the only other year UConn had advanced to the national quarterfinals, the Blue Devils rolled, 101–54. The last meeting came in 1976, with the Huskies falling, 64–59 in New York. Now UConn was looking to de-claw the Beast of the East Regional and advance to its first-ever Final Four. UConn already had conquered Syracuse and Georgetown a total of four times this season; what was one more national NCAA powerhouse?

Duke played with the savvy of a Final Four team in the first half. The Blue Devils' man-to-man forced UConn to turn the ball over twelve times. Meanwhile, with UConn's Sellers still hurting, Abdelnaby was having a career game in the paint. Freshman guard Bobby Hurley repeatedly found the big man open down low, and Abdelnaby responded with 17 points. Duke took a 37–30 lead into the locker room.

The Huskies were 1–5 when trailing at the half; the lone victory came against Georgetown in the Big East tournament. After Laettner started the second half with a pair of free throws, the Huskies responded with a 16–3 run that gave them a 46–42 lead. They had fought back once again, before another national television audience.

UConn maintained the margin and extended it to 69–64 with 3:55 left on Burrell's slam. Fourteen seconds later, though, Burrell (12 points) fouled out of the game. Henderson hit both free throws, and moments later Brian Davis hit a layup to cut the lead to 69–68. Anxious moments indeed. Calhoun called a time-out to reorganize his troops.

Both teams would pick up a steal in the next 1:40, but neither would score. But then Henderson drilled a three with fifty-two seconds left putting Duke up, 71–69. As Young's shot almost buried UConn in the Clemson game, Henderson's shot did the same.

UConn called another time-out to set up the offense. With seventeen seconds left, George

launched a shot that fell short. Bobby Hurley got the rebound and was fouled immediately. He hit the first free throw but missed the second. Smith grabbed the miss and dished to George who drove the length of the floor before returning the ball to Smith. Smith then pulled up from twenty-four feet and nailed a three to tie the score at 72.

The UConn fans could breathe once again. But there were still eight seconds left on the clock—an eternity in this tourney. Hurley launched a shot from the right corner that Sellers swatted out of bounds. Now Duke had but three-tenths of a second to get it done in regulation. Hurley lobbed the inbounds pass to Abdelnaby, who tipped it up. The ball bounced off the rim and finally fell to the floor. UConn was headed for its second overtime game of the season.

UConn had yet another life. Toraino Walker got UConn on the board twenty-one seconds

Scott Burrell leaps past Duke defender, Brian Davis, on his way to a layup.
(Photo by Michael T. Kiernan/*New Haven Register*)

(Photo by Michael T. Kiernan/*New Haven Register*)

The UConn bench prepares for the last play of regulation.

Unfortunately for the Huskies, they could not pull this one off. Christian Laettner's jump shot at the buzzer gave Duke a 79–78 victory.
(Photo by Michael T. Kiernan/*New Haven Register*)

into the overtime, and seconds later he stepped up and intercepted a Duke pass. This was steal number 484 for UConn, two less than Oklahoma's NCAA record.

But UConn could not capitalize on the opportunity, and Henderson responded with a three for a 75–74 Duke lead. George gave UConn the lead back with 2:44 remaining, but Laettner answered right back with a layup of his own.

Neither team would score for the next minute. Then Henefeld drew an offensive foul while guarding Henderson, and went to the line. On the first free throw attempt, Abdelnaby interfered with the ball while it was still in the

149

cylinder and was called for goaltending. One more break for UConn. Henefeld added the next free throw, giving UConn a 78–77 lead.

Henderson took the ball down court and put up a shot that was short. Abdelnaby grabbed the rebound but missed the put-back. UConn grabbed the rebound and appeared to punch its ticket to Denver. But the Huskies missed their shot, giving Duke one last opportunity. Hurley brought the ball up court and fired a pass to Henderson. George got his hands on the ball,

Burrell lays face down on the floor while the Connecticut coaches console each other.
(Photo by Michael T. Kiernan/*New Haven Register*)

but could not gain control. "I was just trying to stay in bounds and keep the ball from trickling out of my hands," George said afterward.

The steal would have brought UConn within one of the NCAA record. Instead, it was Duke's ball with 2.6 seconds left. No one in the arena was sitting down. Laettner passed the ball inbounds to Henderson, who immediately gave it back to Lattener. The sophomore double-pumped in the air, and let it fly from seventeen feet. The ball hit nothing but the bottom of the net. The Blue Devils stormed the court. Tears of sadness flowed in the Connecticut section. The Dream Season was over, a heartbeat away from reaching the Final Four.

Now it was time to reflect on the positives of the season. The first-ever Big East regular-season and tournament titles, a school-record thirty-one wins against just six losses, the top seed in the East Regional and a berth in the Final Eight. Said Calhoun, "I always wanted to coach in a Final Four, but I tell you right now I wouldn't trade this group of kids, and the privilege of coaching them, for 100 Final Fours. I love every one of them. They gave me as much pleasure as a basketball coach deserves. I am so goddamn proud of them."

The team had to sit through hours of traffic on its way home from the Meadowlands, but, when it got back to Storrs, awaiting was perhaps the biggest surprise of the season. As the bus entered the university, the players saw banners hanging from the buildings thanking them for a fantastic season. There were students dangling from tree limbs in front of the Field House trying to get a better view of the crowd, which one student likened to a scene from an Eastern European revolution. There was a radio station blasting music from the back of a truck at a live hookup. There was dancing, cheering, revelry, and pride. One student, perched on top of a theater marquee in the center of campus, high above the rest of the fans, proudly clutched a homemade sign that simply read, "Tate."

The bus pulled up to the Pavilion, where thousands of students had waited for more than three hours. Calhoun took the microphone and thanked the students for their support: "By coming here [tonight], you've mended our bro-

(Photo by Michael T. Kiernan/*New Haven Register*)

Duke's center Alaa Abdelnaby comforts George after UConn's tough loss.

ken hearts." George added, "Treat us the way we are, as people. Don't put us up too far."

In autumn George would head to the NBA, and the Huskies would start yet another season. George's loss would not only be felt in the guard spot, but off the court, too. "It will be hard to replace the intangibles that Tate brought to the table," Tolokan said. "Tate didn't get bothered when we got booed [versus Villanova], because Tate got booed before. He lived with that for four years, he lived with Jim [Calhoun] hollering at him for four years. Now Tate understands why Jim did it, to make him a better, stronger person."

Late in the summer, Calhoun and the Husky faithful received some disappointing news from Nadav Henefeld. It was announced on August 10 that Henefeld would return to Israel to play for Tel Aviv Maccabi of the Israeli professional league. It was reported that Henefeld accepted a contract for $200,000 a year under intense pressure from Israeli officials. Shaken by his departure from Storrs, Henefeld reportedly broke down while relaying his news to Calhoun.

Despite the unexpected loss of Henefeld, the Huskies are still deep in talent and experience. Smith and Gwynn will most likely make up the starting backcourt. The frontcourt will consist of some combination of Cyrulik, Sellers, Burrell, Williams, Lyman DePriest, and Toraino Walker. The Huskies will also add two new players in 1990–91. Gilad Katz, a 6'3" guard and former member of the Israeli National Team, and freshman Shawn Ellison, the 1989–90 Connecticut High School Player of the Year, should make notable contributions to the Huskies.

UConn was picked number one in the 1990–91 pre-season coaches poll. Husky fans can only hope that this poll is more accurate than others in recent years.

Can the Huskies of 1990–91 approach what the 1989–90 edition accomplished? The state of Connecticut can't wait for the magic to begin. In the meantime, hold tight, UConn fans. You might just be in for another ride of your lives.

1989–1990 Game-by-Game
Box Scores

VISITORS Marathon Oil   **Date** Nov. 1, 1989   **Site** Storrs Field House, Storrs, CT

No.	Player Name		Total FG FG	FGA	3-point FG	FGA	FT	FTA	Rebounds Off	Def	Tot	PF	TP	A	TO	BLK	S	MIN
15	Jim Bullock	f	6	11	0	0	3	7	2	4	6	1	15	0	3	0	0	27
25	Darren Fowlkes	f	3	5	2	4	0	0	1	3	4	2	8	1	1	0	1	22
24	Jeff King	c	4	10	0	0	3	4	1	4	5	6	11	1	1	3	1	22
12	Phil Gamble	g	3	9	1	5	2	5	1	5	6	2	9	0	2	0	1	31
14	Eric Turner	g	3	9	0	1	2	4	1	3	4	2	8	8	4	0	1	34
21	Ed Johansen		2	6	0	0	2	2	3	1	4	1	6	1	2	0	0	11
23	Todd May		3	9	1	5	0	0	1	2	3	2	7	2	1	0	0	20
30	Darrin Houston		3	7	2	6	0	0	0	2	2	0	8	3	1	0	1	15
22	Jerome Fitchett		2	3	1	2	1	4	0	0	0	3	6	0	2	0	0	18
	TEAM REBOUNDS (included in Totals)								2	6	8							
	TOTALS		29	69	7	23	13	26	12	30	42	19	78	16	17	3	5	200

TOTAL FG %: 1st Half 19-37 51.4   2nd Half 10-32 31.3   Game 29-69 42.0   Deadball
3-Pt. FG %: 1st Half 4-11 36.4   2nd Half 3-12 25.0   Game 7-23 30.4   Rebounds 8
FT%:   1st Half 3-6 50.0   2nd Half 10-20 50.0   Game 13-26 50.0

HOME Connecticut

No.	Player Name		Total FG FG	FGA	3-point FG	FGA	FT	FTA	Rebounds Off	Def	Tot	PF	TP	A	TO	BLK	S	MIN
23	Lyman DePriest	f	0	3	0	0	0	0	1	2	3	3	0	0	1	0	0	10
24	Scott Burrell	f	2	7	0	4	0	1	1	5	6	1	4	4	0	1	0	22
22	Rod Sellers	c	4	9	0	0	1	2	7	5	12	4	9	1	1	0	1	22
13	Chris Smith	g	12	20	5	8	2	4	1	2	3	1	31	2	1	1	0	27
15	John Gwynn	g	6	8	0	0	1	2	1	0	1	3	13	1	1	0	1	16
20	Murray Williams		5	11	1	3	0	0	2	2	4	0	11	1	0	0	0	12
21	Steve Pikiell		1	3	1	2	0	0	1	0	1	0	3	3	1	0	0	13
32	Tate George		7	13	2	5	0	1	0	0	0	0	16	9	1	0	4	21
55	Dan Cyrulik		0	8	0	1	0	0	1	2	3	5	0	0	1	0	0	17
42	Toraino Walker		1	2	0	0	2	2	0	7	7	2	4	1	1	0	0	17
30	Marc Suhr		4	6	0	0	0	0	1	2	3	1	8	0	1	0	0	14
40	Nadav Henefeld		1	2	0	1	0	0	1	3	4	2	2	1	2	1	1	8
11	Oliver Macklin		0	0	0	0	0	0	0	0	0	0	0	0	0	0	0	1
	TEAM REBOUNDS (included in Totals)								6	3	9							
	TOTALS		43	92	9	24	6	12	23	33	56	22	101	23	11	3	7	200

TOTAL FG %: 1st Half 19-42 45.2   2nd Half 24-50 48.0   Game 43-92 46.7   Deadball
3-Pt. FG %: 1st Half 4-15 26.7   2nd Half 5-9 55.6   Game 9-24 37.5   Rebounds 2
FT%:   1st Half 6-11 54.5   2nd Half 0-1 0.0   Game 6-12 50.0

OFFICIALS: Jack Hannon, John McDonnell, Joe Kepics
Technical Fouls: None
Attendance 4,604 (sellout)

SCORE BY PERIODS	1st H.	2nd H.	OT	OT	FINAL
Marathon Oil	45	33	—	—	78
Connecticut	48	53	—	—	101

155

VISITORS Soviet Union Nat. Team   **Date** Nov. 13, 1989   **Site** Hartford Civic Center

No.	Player Name		Total FG FG	FGA	3-point FG	FGA	FT	FTA	Rebounds Off	Def	Tot	PF	TP	A	TO	BLK	S	MIN
9	Valeri Tikhonenko	f	11	20	4	9	10	11	3	7	10	3	36	2	2	0	2	40
11	Sergei Babenko	f	0	3	0	0	3	4	0	3	3	4	3	0	1	0	0	19
14	Igor Melnik	c	2	5	0	0	3	4	2	2	4	4	7	0	2	0	0	16
4	Gundars Vetra	g	3	8	1	3	3	4	0	3	3	4	10	3	2	0	0	34
5	Tiik Sokk	g	2	8	0	1	6	6	0	2	2	4	10	2	0	0	1	31
8	Oleg Meleshenko		2	7	0	1	4	4	0	2	2	3	8	3	2	0	1	20
10	Yuki Zhukanenko		5	12	2	5	1	2	1	3	4	3	13	0	3	1	4	23
13	Anatoli Yakuhenko		0	0	0	0	0	0	0	1	1	1	0	0	0	0	0	3
00	Georgi Retsov		0	3	0	0	0	4	2	1	3	3	0	0	1	0	0	7
15	Viktor Kulagin		0	2	0	0	0	0	1	1	2	1	0	0	0	0	0	3
6	Vladimir Kuznetsov		0	0	0	0	0	0	0	0	0	0	0	0	0	1	0	4
	TEAM REBOUNDS (included in Totals)								3	1	4							
	TOTALS		25	68	7	19	30	39	12	26	38	30	87	10	13	2	8	200

TOTAL FG %:   1st Half 11-31 35.5   2nd Half 14-37 37.8   Game 25-68 36.8   Deadball
3-Pt. FG %:   1st Half 2-6 33.3   2nd Half 5-13 38.5   Game 7-19 36.8   Rebounds 3
FT%:   1st Half 23-28 82.1   2nd Half 7-11 63.6   Game 30-39 76.9

HOME Connecticut

No.	Player Name		Total FG FG	FGA	3-point FG	FGA	FT	FTA	Rebounds Off	Def	Tot	PF	TP	A	TO	BLK	S	MIN
22	Rod Sellers	f	8	11	0	0	4	5	3	5	8	5	20	0	1	0	0	16
24	Scott Burrell	f	5	10	2	4	1	1	4	4	8	2	13	3	3	1	2	22
55	Dan Cyrulik	c	2	5	1	2	2	2	2	3	5	5	7	1	2	0	0	17
13	Chris Smith	g	9	18	2	6	8	9	0	4	4	1	28	2	3	0	2	34
32	Tate George	g	1	3	0	0	9	13	0	3	3	2	11	6	2	1	0	22
40	Nadav Henefeld		1	4	0	2	2	3	0	3	3	5	4	1	1	0	0	21
15	John Gwynn		2	8	1	3	3	5	1	4	5	0	8	2	1	0	0	15
20	Murray Williams		2	4	0	0	0	0	4	1	5	1	4	3	0	0	1	12
23	Lyman DePriest		0	1	0	0	0	0	2	3	5	2	0	0	2	1	0	12
30	Marc Suhr		0	2	0	0	0	0	1	0	1	2	0	0	0	0	0	6
21	Steve Pikiell		0	1	0	1	0	0	0	0	0	1	0	1	2	0	0	7
42	Toraino Walker		1	2	0	0	0	0	1	4	5	0	2	0	1	0	0	14
31	Tim Pikiell		0	0	0	0	0	0	0	0	0	0	0	0	0	0	0	1
11	Oliver Macklin		0	0	0	0	0	0	0	0	0	0	0	0	0	0	0	1
	TEAM REBOUNDS (included in Totals)								2	2	4							
	TOTALS		31	69	6	18	29	38	20	36	56	26	97	19	18	3	5	200

TOTAL FG %:   1st Half 17-40 42.5   2nd Half 14-29 48.3   Game 31-69 44.9   Deadball
3-Pt. FG %:   1st Half 4-10 40.9   2nd Half 2-8 25.0   Game 6-18 33.3   Rebounds 2
FT%:   1st Half 11-17 64.7   2nd Half 18-21 85.7   Game 29-38 76.3

OFFICIALS: Mickey Crowley, Donnee Gray, Eric Geldart
Technical Fouls: None
Attendance 12,510

SCORE BY PERIODS	1st H.	2nd H.	OT	OT	FINAL
Soviet Union	47	40	—	—	87
Connecticut	49	48	—	—	97

VISITORS Connecticut

Date Nov. 24, 1989   **Site** Sullivan Arena, Anchorage, AK

No.	Player Name		Total FG FG	Total FG FGA	3-point FG	3-point FGA	FT	FTA	Rebounds Off	Rebounds Def	Rebounds Tot	PF	TP	A	TO	BLK	S	MIN
22	Rod Sellers	f	2	6	0	0	0	0	2	0	2	2	4	1	1	1	1	17
24	Scott Burrell	f	3	8	2	3	0	0	3	4	7	2	8	4	1	1	0	28
55	Dan Cyrulik	c	8	13	0	0	2	2	4	5	9	0	18	0	0	0	0	21
13	Chris Smith	g	6	15	4	6	3	4	0	3	3	5	19	4	4	1	2	33
32	Tate George	g	2	10	1	3	3	3	3	1	4	3	8	11	3	0	0	29
15	John Gwynn		5	12	1	4	3	3	0	0	0	1	14	0	1	0	1	21
40	Nadav Henefeld		2	5	0	0	1	2	1	4	5	1	5	2	2	0	4	26
20	Murray Williams		2	4	1	1	0	0	0	1	1	3	5	0	4	0	0	12
23	Lyman DePriest		0	1	0	0	0	0	1	2	3	2	0	1	1	2	1	10
21	Steve Pikiell		0	0	0	0	0	0	0	0	0	1	0	0	1	0	0	2
42	Toraino Walker		0	1	0	0	0	0	1	0	1	0	0	0	0	0	0	1
	TEAM REBOUNDS (included in Totals)										5							
	TOTALS		30	75	9	17	12	14	15	20	40	20	81	23	18	5	9	200

TOTAL FG %:   1st Half 15-40 37.5   2nd Half 15-35 42.9   Game 30-75 40.0   Deadball
3-Pt. FG %:   1st Half 2-5   40.0   2nd Half 7-12 58.3   Game 9-17 52.9   Rebounds 2
FT%:   1st Half 5-6   83.3   2nd Half 7-8   87.5   Game 12-14 85.7

HOME Texas A&M

No.	Player Name		Total FG FG	Total FG FGA	3-point FG	3-point FGA	FT	FTA	Rebounds Off	Rebounds Def	Rebounds Tot	PF	TP	A	TO	BLK	S	MIN
21	David Harris	f	4	9	0	0	1	4	4	7	11	3	9	2	2	3	0	35
24	Lynn Suber	f	11	16	7	8	4	4	0	2	2	1	33	2	4	0	0	28
42	Ray Little	c	2	5	0	2	1	2	3	4	7	3	5	1	1	1	1	30
3	Tony Milton	g	8	22	1	2	9	12	3	1	4	0	26	7	4	0	0	38
14	Freddie Ricks	g	2	3	1	1	0	0	1	5	6	5	5	2	1	1	1	37
11	David Martin		0	0	0	0	0	0	0	0	0	0	0	0	0	0	0	1
23	Brooks Thompson		1	5	1	3	0	0	1	2	3	2	3	3	0	0	1	8
33	Darren Rhea		5	7	1	1	0	0	3	4	7	4	11	0	0	2	1	19
34	David Petersen		0	0	0	0	0	0	0	0	0	0	0	0	0	0	0	3
22	David Williams		0	1	0	0	0	0	0	0	0	0	0	0	0	0	0	1
	TEAM REBOUNDS (included in Totals)										5							
	TOTALS		33	68	11	17	15	22	15	25	45	18	92	17	13	7	4	200

TOTAL FG %:   1st Half 17-31 54.8   2nd Half 16-37 43.2   Game 33-68 48.5   Deadball
3-Pt. FG %:   1st Half 7-11 63.6   2nd Half 4-6   66.7   Game 11-17 64.7   Rebounds 3
FT%:   1st Half 10-13 76.9   2nd Half 5-9   55.6   Game 15-22 68.2

OFFICIALS: Bob Stuvek, Ed Hightower, Glenn Mayborg
Technical Fouls: None
Attendance 4,620

SCORE BY PERIODS	1st H.	2nd H.	OT	OT	FINAL
Connecticut	37	44	—	—	81
Texas A&M	51	41	—	—	92

Second Round—Great Alaska Shootout

VISITORS Auburn   **Date** Nov. 25, 1989   **Site** Sullivan Arena, Anchorage, AK

No.	Player Name		Total FG FG	Total FG FGA	3-point FG	3-point FGA	FT	FTA	Rebounds Off	Rebounds Def	Rebounds Tot	PF	TP	A	TO	BLK	S	MIN
24	Derrick Dennison	f	8	19	1	5	0	1	2	5	7	3	17	10	4	0	3	36
44	Chris Brandt	f	4	6	0	0	4	7	2	5	7	4	12	0	3	0	0	25
34	Robert McKie	c	0	4	0	0	7	8	2	1	3	2	7	1	4	0	1	21
14	Reggie Gallon	g	5	8	4	6	0	0	0	1	1	5	14	6	3	0	3	27
21	Ronnie Battle	g	7	11	6	9	1	2	0	3	3	5	21	2	3	0	1	30
3	Champ Wrencher		0	0	0	0	0	0	0	0	0	0	0	0	4	0	1	6
15	Larry Patrick		0	2	0	2	0	0	0	0	0	0	0	0	0	0	0	2
20	Dustin Hester		0	0	0	0	0	0	0	0	0	0	0	0	4	0	0	8
22	John Caylor		2	8	0	0	0	0	2	1	3	1	4	0	2	0	1	20
23	Rod Joyce		2	2	0	0	0	0	0	2	2	1	4	0	0	0	0	11
31	Richard Smith		0	1	0	0	0	0	0	0	0	0	0	0	0	0	0	2
40	Zane Arnold		1	2	0	0	0	2	2	0	2	2	2	0	0	0	1	7
54	Brian Baumgartner		0	0	0	0	0	0	0	1	1	0	0	0	1	0	0	5
	TEAM REBOUNDS (included in Totals)										2							
	TOTALS		29	63	11	22	12	20	10	19	31	23	81	19	28	0	11	200

TOTAL FG %:   1st Half   9-30   30.0   2nd Half   20-33   60.6   Game   29-63   46.0   Deadball
3-Pt. FG %:   1st Half   2-10   20.0   2nd Half   9-12   75.0   Game   11-22   50.0   Rebounds 3
FT%:   1st Half   7-12   58.3   2nd Half   5-8   62.5   Game   12-20   60.0

HOME Connecticut

No.	Player Name		Total FG FG	Total FG FGA	3-point FG	3-point FGA	FT	FTA	Rebounds Off	Rebounds Def	Rebounds Tot	PF	TP	A	TO	BLK	S	MIN
22	Rod Sellers	f	8	14	0	0	3	10	5	4	9	2	19	0	1	2	2	35
24	Scott Burrell	f	3	8	2	4	5	8	5	4	9	5	13	6	0	0	6	26
55	Dan Cyrulik	c	2	7	0	0	0	0	6	1	7	2	4	1	5	0	0	16
13	Chris Smith	g	4	10	1	3	8	8	0	1	1	2	17	5	5	0	4	26
32	Tate George	g	2	2	1	1	2	3	0	3	3	4	7	4	5	0	0	24
40	Nadav Henefeld		6	7	3	3	1	3	2	2	4	1	16	1	2	1	6	26
15	John Gwynn		7	11	2	5	0	0	0	1	1	0	16	1	2	0	0	22
20	Murray Williams		0	3	0	1	0	0	0	1	1	1	0	0	0	0	0	8
23	Lyman DePriest		0	0	0	0	0	0	0	0	0	0	0	0	1	0	0	1
21	Steve Pikiell		1	2	1	1	0	0	1	1	2	1	3	0	3	0	1	12
42	Toraino Walker		0	0	0	0	0	0	0	1	1	0	0	0	1	0	0	1
30	Marc Suhr		0	1	0	0	0	0	0	0	0	0	0	0	0	0	0	1
31	Tim Pikiell		0	0	0	0	0	0	0	0	0	0	0	0	0	0	0	1
11	Oliver Macklin		0	0	0	0	0	0	0	0	0	0	0	0	0	0	0	1
	TEAM REBOUNDS (included in Totals)										5							
	TOTALS		33	65	10	18	19	32	19	19	43	18	95	18	25	3	19	200

TOTAL FG %:   1st Half 18-36   50.0   2nd Half   15-29   51.7   Game   33-65   50.8   Deadball
3-Pt. FG %:   1st Half   4-11   36.4   2nd Half   6-7   85.7   Game   10-16   55.6   Rebounds 4
FT%:   1st Half   8-15   53.3   2nd Half   11-17   64.7   Game   19-32   59.4

OFFICIALS: Duane Sperbeck, Rick Hartzell, Ed Hightower
Technical Fouls: None
Attendance 3,203

SCORE BY PERIODS	1st H.	2nd H.	OT	OT	FINAL
Auburn	27	54	—	—	81
Connecticut	48	47	—	—	95

VISITORS Connecticut

No.	Player Name		Total FG FG	Total FG FGA	3-point FG	3-point FGA	FT	FTA	Rebounds Off	Rebounds Def	Rebounds Tot	PF	TP	A	TO	BLK	S	MIN
22	Rod Sellers	f	3	9	0	0	4	9	1	4	5	3	10	1	2	1	2	34
24	Scott Burrell	f	4	8	3	5	2	2	2	6	8	3	13	1	2	0	1	32
55	Dan Cyrulik	c	2	5	0	1	1	1	2	2	4	3	5	0	2	1	0	23
13	Chris Smith	g	4	9	1	3	5	5	0	0	0	3	14	4	1	1	0	30
32	Tate George	g	3	7	0	1	2	2	1	2	3	4	8	5	2	0	1	37
40	Nadav Henefeld		3	6	0	2	2	2	1	5	6	4	8	2	4	1	3	26
15	John Gwynn		2	7	1	4	0	0	0	0	0	0	5	1	0	0	0	13
23	Lyman DePriest		0	2	0	0	0	0	1	0	1	1	0	0	0	0	0	4
21	Steve Pikiell		0	0	0	0	0	0	0	0	0	0	0	0	0	0	0	1
	TEAM REBOUNDS (included in Totals)										5							
	TOTALS		21	53	5	16	16	21	8	19	32	21	63	14	13	4	7	200

TOTAL FG %:   1st Half 13-27 48.1   2nd Half 8-26 30.8   Game 21-53 39.6   Deadball
3-Pt. FG %:   1st Half 5-13 38.6   2nd Half 0-3 00.0   Game 5-16 31.3   Rebounds 1
FT%:   1st Half 7-11 63.6   2nd Half 9-10 90.0   Game 16-21 76.2

HOME Florida State

No.	Player Name		Total FG FG	Total FG FGA	3-point FG	3-point FGA	FT	FTA	Rebounds Off	Rebounds Def	Rebounds Tot	PF	TP	A	TO	BLK	S	MIN
31	David White	f	1	2	0	1	0	0	1	2	3	4	2	1	2	1	0	17
45	Michael Polite	f	1	3	0	0	2	4	2	1	3	2	4	0	2	0	1	17
30	Irving Thomas	c	4	10	0	0	7	8	1	5	6	1	15	1	0	1	2	38
20	Aubry Boyd	g	4	7	0	1	0	0	1	5	6	3	8	1	4	0	1	36
22	Tharon Mayes	g	6	16	1	3	6	6	2	4	6	5	19	3	3	0	1	33
4	Chuck Graham		2	7	0	0	0	1	1	1	2	1	4	0	1	0	0	17
10	Chad Copeland		1	1	1	1	0	0	1	0	1	1	3	1	0	0	0	15
11	Lorenzo Hands		0	0	0	0	0	1	0	1	1	0	0	1	0	0	0	3
33	Byron Wells		1	2	0	0	1	2	2	0	2	2	3	0	1	0	0	14
34	Rodney Dobard		1	2	0	0	0	0	2	2	4	2	2	0	1	1	0	10
	TEAM REBOUNDS (included in Totals)										3							
	TOTALS		21	50	2	6	16	22	13	21	37	21	60	8	14	3	5	200

TOTAL FG %:   1st Half 10-22 45.5   2nd Half 11-28 39.3   Game 21-50 42.0   Deadball
3-Pt. FG %:   1st Half 1-3 33.3   2nd Half 1-3 33.3   Game 2-6 33.3   Rebounds 2
FT%:   1st Half 5-10 50.0   2nd Half 11-12 91.7   Game 16-22 72.7

OFFICIALS: Bernard Jackson, Mac Chauvin, Glenn Mayborg
Technical Fouls: None
Attendance 3,179

SCORE BY PERIODS	1st H.	2nd H.	OT	OT	FINAL
Connecticut	38	25	—	—	63
Florida State	26	34	—	—	60

VISITORS Yale Date Nov. 30, 1989 Site Storrs Field House, Storrs, CT

No.	Player Name		Total FG FG	Total FG FGA	3-point FG	3-point FGA	FT	FTA	Rebounds Off	Rebounds Def	Rebounds Tot	PF	TP	A	TO	BLK	S	MIN
20	Travis McCready	f	2	8	0	1	3	4	1	2	3	4	7	1	4	2	0	24
24	Stuart Davies	f	4	8	0	0	3	3	2	5	7	3	11	1	3	0	1	34
52	Casey Cammann	c	1	8	0	0	0	0	3	6	9	4	2	1	2	0	0	26
4	Ed Petersen	g	6	11	3	5	1	2	1	3	4	0	16	1	5	0	2	34
25	Dean Campbell	g	3	7	1	1	0	0	1	1	2	1	7	0	3	1	1	26
34	David Brown		2	4	2	4	1	1	0	0	0	2	7	3	0	0	3	26
22	Todd Trimmer		0	2	0	0	0	0	0	0	0	0	0	1	1	0	0	7
15	Steve Keller		0	1	0	0	0	0	0	0	0	0	0	0	0	0	0	10
10	John Bradsky		0	0	0	0	0	1	0	0	0	0	0	1	1	0	0	6
33	Rob Connolly		0	1	0	1	0	0	0	0	0	0	0	0	1	0	0	5
55	Steve Dave		0	0	0	0	0	0	0	0	0	0	0	0	0	0	0	2
45	Craig Fairfield		0	0	0	0	0	0	0	0	0	0	0	0	0	0	0	1
	TEAM REBOUNDS (included in Totals)								1	1	2							
	TOTALS		18	50	6	12	8	11	9	18	27	14	50	9	20	3	7	200

TOTAL FG %: 1st Half 8-22 36.4 2nd Half 10-28 35.7 Game 18-50 36.0 Deadball
3-Pt. FG %: 1st Half 2-3 66.7 2nd Half 4-9 44.4 Game 6-12 50.0 Rebounds 1
FT%: 1st Half 3-5 60.0 2nd Half 5-6 83.3 Game 8-11 72.7

HOME Connecticut

No.	Player Name		Total FG FG	Total FG FGA	3-point FG	3-point FGA	FT	FTA	Rebounds Off	Rebounds Def	Rebounds Tot	PF	TP	A	TO	BLK	S	MIN
22	Rod Sellers	f	3	5	0	0	2	3	2	2	4	1	8	0	1	2	1	24
24	Scott Burrell	f	5	10	2	3	3	4	4	4	8	3	15	2	0	4	3	32
55	Dan Cyrulik	c	3	3	0	0	0	0	2	1	3	3	6	0	2	0	1	11
13	Chris Smith	g	3	11	1	4	0	0	1	3	4	1	7	5	0	0	0	32
32	Tate George	g	2	5	0	1	2	2	0	2	2	0	6	5	2	0	0	20
40	Nadav Henefeld		6	9	1	2	2	2	0	5	5	3	15	4	3	1	5	25
15	John Gwynn		4	11	2	4	0	0	1	0	1	2	10	0	1	0	1	25
23	Lyman DePriest		2	3	0	0	0	0	2	0	2	0	4	1	2	0	0	13
42	Toraino Walker		1	1	0	0	0	0	1	3	4	0	2	0	2	0	0	8
21	Steve Pikiell		1	1	0	0	1	2	0	1	1	0	3	1	1	0	0	5
30	Marc Suhr		0	0	0	0	0	0	0	0	0	0	0	0	0	0	0	3
11	Oliver Macklin		0	0	0	0	0	0	0	0	0	0	0	0	0	0	0	1
31	Tim Pikiell		0	0	0	0	0	0	0	0	0	0	0	0	0	0	0	1
	TEAM REBOUNDS (included in Totals)								2	3	5							
	TOTALS		30	59	6	14	10	13	15	24	59	13	76	18	14	2	11	200

TOTAL FG %: 1st Half 14-30 46.7 2nd Half 16-29 55.2 Game 30-59 50.8 Deadball
3-Pt. FG %: 1st Half 3-8 37.5 2nd Half 3-6 50.0 Game 6-14 42.9 Rebounds 0
FT%: 1st Half 2-4 50.0 2nd Half 8-9 88.9 Game 10-13 76.9

OFFICIALS: Joe Mingle, Tom Scott, Joe Kepica
Technical Fouls: None
Attendance 4,604 (Sellout)

SCORE BY PERIODS	1st H.	2nd H.	OT	OT	FINAL
Yale	21	29			50
Connecticut	33	43			76

VISITORS Howard **Date** Dec. 2, 1989 **Site** Storrs Field House, Storrs, CT

No.	Player Name		Total FG		3-point		FT	FTA	Rebounds			PF	TP	A	TO	BLK	S	MIN
			FG	FGA	FG	FGA			Off	Def	Tot							
11	Keith Kirvin	f	1	7	0	0	0	2	2	4	6	3	2	3	5	0	0	29
23	Guy Owens	f	4	9	0	1	2	3	1	3	4	1	10	0	3	1	1	26
52	Charles Chase	c	3	4	0	0	0	0	1	1	2	3	6	0	2	0	0	15
10	Milton Bynum	g	2	7	1	3	0	1	0	3	3	2	5	0	0	0	1	21
15	Martin Huckaby	g	4	13	3	6	5	6	0	2	2	1	16	5	4	0	2	31
45	Tyrone Powell		2	8	0	0	1	2	3	5	8	0	5	0	0	0	0	23
21	Tracy King		0	1	0	0	0	0	0	0	0	0	0	0	0	1	0	6
24	Ronnie Gibbs		0	1	0	0	2	2	1	0	1	1	2	1	0	0	1	8
29	Milan Brown		3	7	2	5	2	2	0	1	1	2	10	2	3	0	2	20
31	Robert Riddick		1	1	0	0	0	2	1	1	2	0	2	0	1	0	1	8
42	Derek Faison		0	1	0	0	0	0	0	0	0	0	0	0	0	0	0	3
50	Kelsey Sturdivant		0	0	0	0	1	3	0	0	0	0	1	0	0	0	0	10
	TEAM REBOUNDS (included in Totals)								3	0	3							
	TOTALS		20	59	6	15	13	23	12	20	32	13	59	11	18	2	8	200

TOTAL FG %: 1st Half 10-33 30.3 2nd Half 10-26 38.5 Game 20-59 33.5 Deadball
3-Pt. FG %: 1st Half 2-7 28.6 2nd Half 4-8 50.0 Game 6-15 40.0 Rebounds 4
FT%: 1st Half 2-7 28.6 2nd Half 11-16 68.8 Game 13-23 56.5

HOME Connecticut

No.	Player Name		Total FG		3-point		FT	FTA	Rebounds			PF	TP	A	TO	BLK	S	MIN
			FG	FGA	FG	FGA			Off	Def	Tot							
22	Rod Sellers	f	5	8	0	0	1	3	4	4	8	2	11	0	3	2	1	20
24	Scott Burrell	f	3	13	0	4	0	0	1	3	4	1	6	3	2	0	2	30
55	Dan Cyrulik	c	2	8	0	1	0	0	5	10	15	2	4	0	2	0	2	24
13	Chris Smith	g	4	12	3	5	0	0	0	0	0	3	11	9	0	0	1	30
32	Tate George	g	6	9	1	1	2	2	2	4	6	1	15	5	1	1	2	26
15	John Gwynn		6	10	1	1	0	0	2	0	2	1	13	0	0	0	0	16
40	Nadav Henefeld		3	4	1	2	0	0	2	3	5	0	7	1	2	1	2	16
23	Lyman DePriest		1	4	0	0	1	2	3	3	6	1	3	0	2	0	0	11
42	Toraino Walker		2	2	0	0	0	1	1	5	6	4	4	1	2	0	1	13
21	Steve Pikiell		0	0	0	0	0	0	0	0	0	0	0	0	3	0	0	6
30	Marc Suhr		1	2	0	0	0	0	0	0	0	0	2	0	2	0	0	3
11	Oliver Macklin		1	1	0	0	0	0	1	0	1	0	2	0	0	0	0	3
31	Tim Pikiell		0	0	0	0	0	0	0	0	0	1	0	0	0	0	0	2
	TEAM REBOUNDS (included in Totals)								0	1	1							
	TOTALS		34	73	6	14	4	8	21	33	54	16	78	19	19	4	11	200

TOTAL FG %: 1st Half 18-36 50.0 2nd Half 16-37 43.2 Game 34-73 46.6 Deadball
3-Pt. FG %: 1st Half 5-11 45.5 2nd Half 1-3 33.3 Game 6-14 42.9 Rebounds 2
FT%: 1st Half 1-3 33.3 2nd Half 3-5 60.0 Game 4-8 50.0

OFFICIALS: John Cahill, Don Winterton, Alonzo Holloway
Technical Fouls: None
Attendance 4,604 (Sellout)

SCORE BY PERIODS	1st H.	2nd H.	OT	OT	FINAL
Howard	24	35	—	—	59
Connecticut	42	36	—	—	78

VISITORS Connecticut **Date** Dec. 4, 1989 **Site** Hartford CC, Hartford, CT

No.	Player Name		Total FG FG	Total FG FGA	3-point FG	3-point FGA	FT	FTA	Rebounds Off	Rebounds Def	Rebounds Tot	PF	TP	A	TO	BLK	S	MIN
22	Rod Sellers	f	2	6	0	0	6	12	3	2	5	4	10	0	1	0	3	26
24	Scott Burrell	f	4	9	3	6	0	0	4	4	8	1	11	2	3	2	4	32
55	Dan Cyrulik	c	4	9	0	0	1	2	3	3	6	1	9	1	3	1	0	20
13	Chris Smith	g	9	19	3	7	1	1	4	1	5	2	22	5	3	0	0	29
32	Tate George	g	2	4	0	1	0	1	1	2	3	3	4	5	2	0	3	26
40	Nadav Henefeld		3	8	2	3	3	4	3	4	7	2	11	3	0	0	5	24
15	John Gwynn		4	9	1	5	1	2	1	1	2	2	10	5	2	0	2	21
23	Lyman DePriest		3	4	0	0	1	2	1	1	2	2	7	0	2	0	1	11
42	Toraino Walker		0	0	0	0	1	2	0	1	1	0	1	0	1	1	0	4
21	Steve Pikiell		1	1	0	0	0	0	0	0	0	0	2	1	0	0	0	4
30	Marc Suhr		0	1	0	0	0	1	0	0	0	1	0	0	0	0	0	2
11	Oliver Macklin		0	1	0	0	0	0	0	1	1	1	0	0	0	0	0	1
	TEAM REBOUNDS (included in Totals)								2	3	5							
	TOTALS		32	71	9	22	14	27	22	23	45	19	87	22	17	4	18	200

TOTAL FG %: 1st Half 17-38 44.7 2nd Half 15-33 45.5 Game 32-71 45.1 Deadball
3-Pt. FG %: 1st Half 5-14 35.7 2nd Half 4-8 50.0 Game 9-22 40.9 Rebounds 8
FT%: 1st Half 10-13 76.9 2nd Half 4-14 28.6 Game 14-27 51.9

HOME Maryland

No.	Player Name		Total FG FG	Total FG FGA	3-point FG	3-point FGA	FT	FTA	Rebounds Off	Rebounds Def	Rebounds Tot	PF	TP	A	TO	BLK	S	MIN
25	Tony Massenburg	f	4	9	0	0	3	4	4	5	9	4	11	1	5	2	2	37
32	Jerrod Mustaf	f	10	18	4	4	1	3	2	3	5	1	25	0	5	0	0	31
43	Cedric Lewis	c	0	1	0	0	0	0	0	2	2	1	0	0	2	1	1	15
11	Teyon McCoy	g	1	5	1	4	2	2	0	1	1	4	5	4	3	0	2	24
42	Walt Williams	g	1	9	1	3	1	2	2	3	5	4	4	3	6	1	2	33
22	Kevin McLinton		2	2	0	0	0	0	0	2	2	4	4	5	3	0	1	18
30	Rodney Walker		1	2	0	0	0	0	0	1	1	0	2	0	1	0	0	9
14	Jesse Martin		1	3	0	0	0	0	0	0	0	0	2	0	0	1	0	4
40	Vincent Broadnax		1	1	0	0	1	3	0	0	0	1	3	0	1	0	0	11
33	Evers Burns		2	4	0	0	1	4	1	2	3	0	5	0	0	1	0	11
5	Mitch Kessoff		0	1	0	0	2	2	0	0	0	1	2	2	1	0	0	3
21	Curley Young		1	2	0	0	0	0	1	0	1	0	2	0	0	0	0	3
13	Matt Kaluzienski		0	0	0	0	0	0	0	0	0	1	0	0	0	0	0	1
	TEAM REBOUNDS (included in Totals)								7	2	9							
	TOTALS		24	57	6	11	11	20	17	21	38	21	65	15	27	6	8	200

TOTAL FG %: 1st Half 13-27 48.1 2nd Half 11-30 36.7 Game 24-57 42.1 Deadball
3-Pt. FG %: 1st Half 2-4 50.0 2nd Half 4-7 57.1 Game 6-11 54.5 Rebounds 3
FT%: 1st Half 5-9 55.6 2nd Half 6-11 55.5 Game 11-20 55.0

OFFICIALS: Judy Silvester, Frank Scagliotta, Stanley Rote
Technical Fouls: None
Attendance 10,174

SCORE BY PERIODS	1st H.	2nd H.	OT	OT	FINAL
Connecticut	49	38	—	—	87
Maryland	33	32	—	—	65

VISITORS Hartford **Date** Dec. 7, 1989 **Site** Hartford CC, Hartford, CT

No.	Player Name		FG	FGA	FG	FGA	FT	FTA	Off	Def	Tot	PF	TP	A	TO	BLK	S	MIN
			Total FG		3-point				Rebounds									
11	David Thompson	f	3	8	0	1	0	0	1	2	3	1	6	3	8	1	4	38
30	Lamont Middleton	f	7	10	0	0	3	4	2	5	7	4	17	1	2	0	1	37
13	Larry Griffiths	c	3	10	0	0	4	6	4	5	9	3	10	2	4	0	1	31
3	Alexander Jones	g	1	3	0	2	0	0	0	3	3	2	2	2	6	0	2	24
10	Ron Moye	g	5	13	1	6	0	2	1	1	2	2	11	0	4	0	0	38
24	Donnail Diggs		2	3	0	0	0	1	1	2	3	2	4	0	4	0	3	16
42	Vin Baker		2	6	0	0	0	1	1	0	1	4	4	0	0	0	0	11
32	Mark Matthews		0	0	0	0	0	0	0	1	1	0	0	0	0	0	0	3
15	Paul Spence		0	1	0	1	0	0	0	1	1	0	0	0	0	0	0	2
	TEAM REBOUNDS (included in Totals)								2	4	6							
	TOTALS		23	54	1	10	7	14	12	24	36	18	54	8	28	1	11	200

TOTAL FG %: 1st Half 9-26 34.6 2nd Half 14-28 50.0 Game 23-54 42.6 Deadball
3-Pt. FG %: 1st Half 0-4 00.0 2nd Half 1-6 16.7 Game 1-10 10.0 Rebounds 2
FT%: 1st Half 3-6 50.0 2nd Half 4-8 50.0 Game 7-14 50.0

HOME Connecticut

No.	Player Name		FG	FGA	FG	FGA	FT	FTA	Off	Def	Tot	PF	TP	A	TO	BLK	S	MIN
			Total FG		3-point				Rebounds									
22	Rod Sellers	f	5	6	0	0	4	4	3	3	6	4	14	1	3	1	1	23
24	Scott Burrell	f	1	9	0	5	1	2	2	5	7	3	3	0	1	2	1	30
55	Dan Cyrulik	c	2	9	0	0	0	0	3	6	9	2	4	0	2	2	2	20
13	Chris Smith	g	6	10	1	3	3	3	0	0	0	1	16	3	4	0	4	32
32	Tate George	g	5	10	0	0	2	5	1	1	2	1	12	6	4	0	4	25
40	Nadav Henefeld		4	7	0	0	0	0	2	5	7	2	8	1	2	1	4	23
15	John Gwynn		5	11	1	2	0	0	0	1	1	2	11	4	2	0	3	25
23	Lyman DePriest		2	2	0	0	4	6	0	0	0	0	8	1	2	0	5	17
42	Toraino Walker		1	1	0	0	0	0	1	1	2	0	2	0	0	0	0	3
21	Steve Pikiell		0	0	0	0	1	3	0	0	0	0	1	0	1	0	0	2
	TEAM REBOUNDS (included in Totals)								2	2	4							
	TOTALS		31	65	2	10	15	23	14	24	38	15	79	16	21	6	24	200

TOTAL FG %: 1st Half 15-30 50.0 2nd Half 16-35 45.7 Game 31-65 47.7 Deadball
3-Pt. FG %: 1st Half 2-6 33.3 2nd Half 0-4 00.0 Game 2-10 20.0 Rebounds 4
FT%: 1st Half 3-3 100 2nd Half 12-20 60.0 Game 15-23 65.2

OFFICIALS: Joe Mingle, Frank Scagliotta, Sean Corbin
Technical Fouls: Hartford Bench
Attendance 13,102

SCORE BY PERIODS	1st H.	2nd H.	OT	OT	FINAL
Hartford	21	33	—	—	54
Connecticut	35	44	—	—	79

VISITORS Maine   **Date** Dec. 9, 1989   **Site** Storrs Field House, Storrs, CT

No.	Player Name		Total FG		3-point		FT	FTA	Rebounds			PF	TP	A	TO	BLK	S	MIN
			FG	FGA	FG	FGA			Off	Def	Tot							
24	Dean Smith	f	6	9	0	0	1	3	2	1	3	1	13	1	0	0	0	32
25	Francois Bouchard	f	2	5	0	0	2	2	0	3	3	1	6	0	4	1	0	23
32	Curtis Robertson	c	2	3	0	0	1	2	0	4	4	3	5	1	3	0	1	22
13	Marty Higgins	g	1	5	0	2	0	0	0	0	0	2	2	5	4	0	1	31
15	Derrick Hodge	g	2	14	2	6	4	4	4	2	6	1	10	4	3	1	4	29
10	Todd Hanson		0	2	0	1	1	2	1	0	1	0	1	1	1	0	0	8
22	Guy Gomis		1	1	0	0	0	0	1	1	2	1	2	0	2	0	0	9
21	Shelton Kerry		4	0	3	6	1	4	2	2	4	3	12	0	1	0	0	17
23	Pat Harrington		0	3	0	3	2	2	0	1	1	0	2	0	4	0	0	10
31	Dan Hillman		1	2	0	0	0	0	1	1	2	3	2	1	2	0	1	16
11	Bryan Tilton		0	0	0	0	0	0	0	1	1	0	0	0	0	0	0	3
	TEAM REBOUNDS (included in Totals)								2	3	5							
	TOTALS		19	52	5	18	12	19	13	19	32	15	55	13	24	2	7	200

TOTAL FG %:   1st Half 6-19 31.6   2nd Half 13-33 39.4   Game 19-52 36.5   Deadball
3-Pt. FG %:   1st Half 2-5 40.0   2nd Half 3-13 23.1   Game 5-18 27.8   Rebounds 2
FT%:   1st Half 8-12 66.7   2nd Half 4-7 52.1   Game 12-19 63.2

HOME Connecticut

No.	Player Name		Total FG		3-point		FT	FTA	Rebounds			PF	TP	A	TO	BLK	S	MIN
			FG	FGA	FG	FGA			Off	Def	Tot							
22	Rod Sellers	f	11	12	0	0	0	0	5	2	7	0	22	2	3	0	1	24
24	Scott Burrell	f	1	4	1	2	0	0	0	4	4	4	3	4	0	1	3	21
55	Dan Cyrulik	c	4	10	0	1	0	0	3	4	7	1	8	0	1	0	0	21
13	Chris Smith	g	6	11	0	2	2	3	0	1	1	3	14	7	2	0	0	25
32	Tate George	g	4	7	1	2	1	1	2	0	2	1	10	8	1	0	3	23
15	John Gwynn		5	13	0	3	1	2	2	1	3	1	11	1	2	0	3	20
40	Nadav Henefeld		4	11	2	6	2	4	5	6	11	3	12	2	0	0	4	20
23	Lyman DePriest		1	4	0	0	0	0	1	0	1	1	2	1	1	1	0	13
21	Steve Pikiell		0	3	0	0	1	2	1	1	2	0	1	1	0	0	1	15
42	Toraino Walker		4	5	0	0	0	2	3	3	6	0	8	1	1	0	0	13
30	Marc Suhr		1	2	0	0	0	0	1	0	1	0	2	0	0	0	0	3
11	Oliver Macklin		1	2	0	0	0	0	0	1	1	1	2	0	0	0	0	1
31	Tim Pikiell		0	0	0	0	0	0	0	0	0	0	0	0	0	0	0	1
	TEAM REBOUNDS (included in Totals)								3	2	5							
	TOTALS		42	84	4	16	7	14	26	25	51	15	95	27	11	2	15	200

TOTAL FG %:   1st Half 21-41 51.2   2nd Half 21-43 48.8   Game 42-84 50.0   Deadball
3-Pt. FG %:   1st Half 0-5 00.0   2nd Half 4-11 36.4   Game 4-16 25.0   Rebounds 4
FT%:   1st Half 2-4 50.0   2nd Half 5-10 50.0   Game 7-14 50.0

OFFICIALS: Mickey Crowley, Jack Hannon, Michael Kitts
Technical Fouls: Maine Bench
Attendance 4,604 (Sellout)

SCORE BY PERIODS	1st H.	2nd H.	OT	OT	FINAL
Maine	22	33	—	—	55
Connecticut	44	51	—	—	95

VISITORS Villanova (5-3, 1-0)   **Date** Dec. 12, 1989   **Site** Hartford CC, Hartford, CT

No.	Player Name		Total FG FG	Total FG FGA	3-point FG	3-point FGA	FT	FTA	Rebounds Off	Rebounds Def	Rebounds Tot	PF	TP	A	TO	BLK	S	MIN
35	Rodney Taylor	f	3	3	0	0	4	7	0	6	6	5	10	1	2	0	1	29
44	Arron Bain	f	1	6	0	3	4	4	0	3	3	2	6	2	6	0	0	21
33	Tom Greis	c	4	6	0	0	4	6	3	10	13	0	12	1	7	3	0	34
15	Chris Walker	g	2	5	0	1	2	3	0	2	2	3	6	3	3	0	2	29
24	Greg Woodard	g	5	8	3	5	4	4	1	1	2	4	17	1	4	1	0	39
14	Lance Miller		3	7	0	0	3	3	0	6	6	2	9	2	0	0	0	29
32	Marc Dowdell		2	5	0	0	0	0	0	2	2	2	4	0	0	0	0	15
21	Calvin Byrd		0	0	0	0	0	0	0	0	0	0	0	0	3	0	0	3
41	James Bryson		0	0	0	0	0	0	0	0	0	0	0	0	0	0	0	1
	TEAM REBOUNDS (included in Totals)								1	4	5							
	TOTALS		20	40	3	9	21	27	5	34	39	18	64	10	25	4	3	200

TOTAL FG %:   1st Half 11-21 52.4   2nd Half 9-19 47.4   Game 20-40 50.0   Deadball
3-Pt. FG %:   1st Half 2-4 50.0   2nd Half 1-5 20.0   Game 3-9 33.3   Rebounds 1
FT%:   1st Half 7-9 77.8   2nd Half 14-18 77.8   Game 21-27 77.8

HOME Connecticut (7-2, 0-1)

No.	Player Name		Total FG FG	Total FG FGA	3-point FG	3-point FGA	FT	FTA	Rebounds Off	Rebounds Def	Rebounds Tot	PF	TP	A	TO	BLK	S	MIN
22	Rod Sellers	f	1	3	0	0	1	5	0	2	2	2	3	0	1	1	1	24
24	Scott Burrell	f	7	18	2	6	2	6	4	4	8	6	18	2	2	2	3	37
55	Dan Cyrulik	c	5	12	1	2	2	4	4	3	7	5	13	1	2	0	0	23
13	Chris Smith	g	5	16	0	6	2	3	3	0	3	2	12	4	3	1	0	38
32	Tate George	g	3	7	0	1	0	0	1	3	4	1	6	2	2	1	3	24
40	Nadav Henefeld		1	4	1	2	0	0	1	5	6	5	3	1	1	0	2	28
15	John Gwynn		1	8	0	3	0	0	1	1	2	2	2	1	1	0	1	14
23	Lyman DePriest		0	1	0	0	0	0	0	0	0	0	0	0	0	0	0	8
21	Steve Pikiell		0	1	0	0	0	0	0	0	0	0	0	1	0	0	0	4
	TEAM REBOUNDS (included in Totals)								2	5	7							
	TOTALS		23	70	4	20	7	18	16	23	39	23	57	12	12	5	10	200

TOTAL FG %:   1st Half 7-34 20.6   2nd Half 16-36 44.4   Game 23-70 32.9   Deadball
3-Pt. FG %:   1st Half 1-10 10.0   2nd Half 3-10 30.0   Game 4-20 20.0   Rebounds 5
FT%:   1st Half 1-8 12.5   2nd Half 6-10 60.0   Game 7-18 38.9

OFFICIALS: Jim Howell, Jim Burr, John Moreau
Technical Fouls: None
Attendance 14,947

SCORE BY PERIODS	1st H.	2nd H.	OT	OT	FINAL
Villanova	31	33	—	—	64
Connecticut	16	41	—	—	57

VISITORS Southern Connecticut   **Date** Dec. 23, 1989   **Site** Storrs FH, Storrs, CT

No.	Player Name		Total FG FG	FGA	3-point FG	FGA	FT	FTA	Rebounds Off	Def	Tot	PF	TP	A	TO	BLK	S	MIN
33	Aaron Martin	f	2	7	0	1	3	6	2	2	4	1	7	0	5	0	2	31
34	Rich Radicioni	f	4	9	2	3	1	2	2	2	4	5	11	1	2	0	1	20
40	Jim Rourke	c	3	7	0	0	2	2	4	0	4	2	8	0	4	0	0	39
14	Phillippe Valentin	g	1	8	1	6	0	0	2	1	3	2	3	4	4	0	4	35
24	Matt D'Amico	g	1	4	1	3	0	0	0	0	0	2	3	2	2	0	2	26
23	Jeff Kimbrough		0	4	0	3	0	0	0	0	0	1	0	1	0	0	0	13
20	James Hollis		0	3	0	0	0	0	0	3	3	1	0	0	0	0	0	8
44	Pat Good		2	10	1	6	0	0	0	1	1	1	5	1	4	0	0	17
32	Brian Hipsky		0	0	0	0	0	0	0	0	0	1	0	0	1	0	0	4
42	Phil Buccni		0	1	0	0	0	0	0	0	0	0	0	0	1	1	0	5
10	Larnell Satchell		0	0	0	0	0	0	0	0	0	0	0	0	0	0	0	1
22	Joe Nappo		0	0	0	0	0	0	0	0	0	0	0	0	0	0	0	1
	TEAM REBOUNDS (included in Totals)								1	1	2							
	TOTALS		13	53	5	22	6	10	11	10	21	16	37	9	23	1	9	200

TOTAL FG %:   1st Half 9-24 37.5   2nd Half 4-29 13.8   Game 13-53 24.5   Deadball
3-Pt. FG %:   1st Half 4-6   66.7   2nd Half 1-16 6.3   Game 5-22   22.7   Rebounds 3
FT%:   1st Half 3-4   75.0   2nd Half 3-6   50.0   Game 6-10   60.0

HOME Connecticut (8-2)

No.	Player Name		Total FG FG	FGA	3-point FG	FGA	FT	FTA	Rebounds Off	Def	Tot	PF	TP	A	TO	BLK	S	MIN
22	Rod Sellers	f	4	4	0	0	0	2	2	5	7	2	8	0	0	1	1	18
24	Scott Burrell	f	3	6	1	1	2	2	5	3	8	2	9	0	1	2	1	21
55	Dan Cyrulik	c	1	1	0	0	0	0	0	1	1	1	2	0	0	0	0	13
13	Chris Smith	g	7	12	3	7	3	5	2	0	2	0	20	5	3	2	0	22
32	Tate George	g	6	11	0	2	0	0	0	2	2	0	12	9	0	0	1	23
15	John Gwynn		6	14	2	7	2	2	2	2	4	0	16	0	1	0	2	17
40	Nadav Henefeld		3	6	3	5	0	0	2	6	8	2	9	6	4	3	6	23
20	Murray Williams		3	5	0	1	1	2	1	1	2	0	7	0	1	0	0	16
42	Toraino Walker		2	4	0	0	1	2	9	1	10	1	5	2	1	0	1	15
21	Steve Pikiell		1	5	1	5	0	0	0	1	1	1	3	1	1	0	1	15
30	Marc Suhr		2	5	0	0	0	1	2	3	5	0	4	0	0	0	0	9
11	Oliver Macklin		1	2	1	2	2	2	0	1	1	0	5	0	1	0	1	5
31	Tim Pikiell		0	0	0	0	0	0	0	1	1	0	0	1	0	0	0	3
	TEAM REBOUNDS (included in Totals)								4	2	6							
	TOTALS		39	75	11	30	11	18	29	29	58	9	100	23	13	8	14	200

TOTAL FG %:   1st Half 20-46 43.5   2nd Half 19-29 65.5   Game 39-75 52.0   Deadball
3-Pt. FG %:   1st Half 8-21   38.1   2nd Half 3-9   33.3   Game 11-30 36.7   Rebounds 5
FT%:   1st Half 4-6   66.7   2nd Half 7-12   58.3   Game 11-18 61.1

OFFICIALS: Joe Mingle, Sean Corbin, Bob Madigan
Technical Fouls: SCSU Bench
Attendance 4,604 (Sellout)

SCORE BY PERIODS	1st H.	2nd H.	OT	OT	FINAL
SCSU	25	12	—	—	37
Connecticut	52	48	—	—	100

VISITORS St. Joseph's   **Date** Dec. 29, 1989   **Site** Hartford CC, Hartford, CT

No.	Player Name		Total FG FG	Total FG FGA	3-point FG	3-point FGA	FT	FTA	Rebounds Off	Rebounds Def	Rebounds Tot	PF	TP	A	TO	BLK	S	MIN
25	Richard Stewart	f	2	6	0	1	0	0	0	1	1	5	4	2	3	1	2	24
34	Marlon Miller	f	4	14	0	1	7	10	1	2	3	2	15	1	1	0	2	33
31	Ron Vercruyssen	c	3	9	0	0	0	1	4	2	6	5	6	1	3	0	1	24
10	Chris Gardler	g	1	4	0	2	4	4	0	6	6	1	6	3	4	0	1	33
22	Craig Amos	g	4	13	2	4	6	7	3	7	10	4	16	2	5	1	1	32
14	Ray Washington		1	2	0	0	0	0	1	1	2	2	2	2	2	0	3	22
21	Brian Daly		1	5	0	3	0	0	0	2	2	2	2	0	1	0	0	9
13	Eddie Malloy		2	7	0	1	0	0	1	2	3	3	4	0	1	0	0	13
41	Mor Naaman		1	3	0	0	1	1	2	3	5	1	3	0	1	0	0	10
	TEAM REBOUNDS (included in Totals)								1	2	3							
	TOTALS		19	63	2	12	18	23	13	28	41	25	58	11	21	2	10	200

TOTAL FG %: 1st Half 8-29 27.6   2nd Half 11-34 32.4   Game 19-63 30.2   Deadball
3-Pt. FG %: 1st Half 2-3 66.7   2nd Half 0-9 00.0   Game 2-12 16.7   Rebounds 2
FT%:   1st Half 8-10 80.0   2nd Half 10-13 76.9   Game 18-23 78.3

HOME Connecticut

No.	Player Name		Total FG FG	Total FG FGA	3-point FG	3-point FGA	FT	FTA	Rebounds Off	Rebounds Def	Rebounds Tot	PF	TP	A	TO	BLK	S	MIN
24	Scott Burrell	f	1	2	0	1	1	2	0	5	5	4	3	0	1	1	1	18
40	Nadav Henefeld	f	4	5	1	2	0	2	1	3	4	3	9	2	2	0	5	21
22	Rod Sellers	c	2	5	0	0	5	8	4	5	9	3	9	0	2	0	0	23
13	Chris Smith	g	6	15	3	8	4	6	0	2	2	1	19	7	1	1	2	30
32	Tate George	g	5	9	1	2	3	4	1	2	3	1	14	6	2	0	0	26
20	Murray Williams		2	6	0	1	4	9	4	5	9	2	8	1	0	0	1	23
15	John Gwynn		5	10	0	2	0	3	0	2	2	2	10	1	1	0	3	16
55	Dan Cyrulik		3	6	0	0	0	0	4	1	5	3	6	0	3	0	0	15
23	Lyman DePriest		0	1	0	0	1	2	0	3	3	0	1	1	2	0	2	7
42	Toraino Walker		0	0	0	0	1	2	0	0	0	1	1	0	0	0	0	7
21	Steve Pikiell		0	1	0	1	1	3	0	1	1	0	1	1	2	0	0	6
30	Marc Suhr		0	1	0	0	0	0	0	1	1	0	0	0	1	0	0	3
31	Tim Pikiell		0	0	0	0	0	0	0	1	1	0	0	0	0	0	0	2
11	Oliver Macklin		1	2	0	0	0	0	0	1	1	0	2	0	0	0	0	3
	TEAM REBOUNDS (included in Totals)								2	1	3							
	TOTALS		29	63	5	17	20	41	16	33	49	20	83	19	17	2	14	200

TOTAL FG %: 1st Half 14-31 45.2   2nd Half 15-32 46.9   Game 29-63 46.0   Deadball
3-Pt. FG %: 1st Half 4-11 36.4   2nd Half 1-6   16.7   Game 5-17 29.4   Rebounds 12
FT%:   1st Half 11-20 55.0   2nd Half 9-21 42.9   Game 20-41 48.8

OFFICIALS: Gene Monje, Rich Sanfillipo, Bruce Shapiro
Technical Fouls: None
Attendance 13,682

SCORE BY PERIODS	1st H.	2nd H.	OT	OT	FINAL
St. Joseph's	26	32	—	—	58
Connecticut	43	40	—	—	83

VISITORS Mississippi State   **Date** Dec. 30, 1989   **Site** Hartford CC, Hartford, CT

No.	Player Name		Total FG FG	Total FG FGA	3-point FG	3-point FGA	FT	FTA	Rebounds Off	Rebounds Def	Rebounds Tot	PF	TP	A	TO	BLK	S	MIN
21	Cameron Burns	f	8	15	0	0	3	8	3	6	9	3	19	0	2	0	1	38
23	Greg Carter	f	7	11	2	2	1	1	6	2	8	3	17	3	0	0	1	35
33	Carl Nichols	c	1	2	0	0	2	3	0	1	1	2	4	0	2	0	0	7
20	Doug Hartsfield	g	3	9	2	7	0	0	1	6	7	5	8	6	8	0	0	38
22	Tony Watts	g	5	15	3	10	1	1	0	4	4	2	14	2	3	1	2	32
10	Brad Smith		0	1	0	0	0	0	0	0	0	1	0	1	3	1	0	4
30	Todd Merritt		0	4	0	1	3	4	0	1	1	2	3	0	2	0	0	35
25	Robert Woodard		1	1	1	1	0	0	0	1	1	5	3	0	1	0	2	10
13	Mike Granato		0	1	0	0	0	0	0	0	0	1	0	1	0	0	0	1
	TEAM REBOUNDS (included in Totals)								5	1	6							
	TOTALS		25	59	8	21	10	17	15	22	37	24	68	13	21	2	6	200

TOTAL FG %:   1st Half 12-25   48.0   2nd Half 13-34   38.2   Game 25-59   42.4   Deadball
3-Pt. FG %:   1st Half 2-4   50.0   2nd Half 6-17   35.3   Game 8-21   38.1   Rebounds 2
FT%:   1st Half 3-5   60.0   2nd Half 7-12   58.3   Game 10-17   58.8

HOME Connecticut

No.	Player Name		Total FG FG	Total FG FGA	3-point FG	3-point FGA	FT	FTA	Rebounds Off	Rebounds Def	Rebounds Tot	PF	TP	A	TO	BLK	S	MIN
24	Scott Burrell	f	5	8	0	1	1	3	1	3	4	3	11	2	1	0	0	33
40	Nadav Henefeld	f	7	11	0	1	3	4	3	3	6	3	17	3	3	1	6	31
22	Rod Sellers	c	2	3	0	0	2	2	3	1	4	4	6	0	0	1	1	13
13	Chris Smith	g	7	15	0	2	0	1	2	3	5	1	14	4	3	0	3	33
32	Tate George	g	5	9	0	1	3	5	0	6	6	1	13	8	2	0	5	34
55	Dan Cyrulik		0	3	0	1	0	0	0	2	2	0	0	0	1	0	0	14
15	John Gwynn		6	7	0	0	2	2	1	0	1	0	14	0	1	0	0	14
20	Murray Williams		3	8	0	0	3	4	2	1	3	1	9	3	0	0	2	19
42	Toraino Walker		0	0	0	0	0	0	0	0	0	0	0	0	0	0	0	2
23	Lyman DePriest		0	0	0	0	0	0	0	0	0	2	0	0	0	0	0	3
11	Oliver Macklin		0	0	0	0	0	1	0	0	0	0	0	0	0	0	0	1
30	Marc Suhr		0	0	0	0	0	0	0	0	0	0	0	0	0	0	0	1
31	Tim Pikiell		0	0	0	0	0	1	0	1	1	0	0	0	0	0	0	1
21	Steve Pikiell		0	0	0	0	0	0	0	0	0	0	0	0	0	0	0	1
	TEAM REBOUNDS (included in Totals)								2	4	6							
	TOTALS		35	64	0	6	14	23	14	24	38	15	84	20	11	2	17	200

TOTAL FG %:   1st Half 19-34   55.9   2nd Half 15-30   50.0   Game 35-64   54.7   Deadball
3-Pt. FG %:   1st Half 0-2   00.0   2nd Half 0-4   00.0   Game 0-6   00.0   Rebounds 2
FT%:   1st Half 8-11   72.7   2nd Half 6-12   50.0   Game 14-23   60.0

OFFICIALS: Jack Hannon, Donnee Grey, Frank Scagliotta
Technical Fouls: None
Attendance 14,115

SCORE BY PERIODS	1st H.	2nd H.	OT	OT	FINAL
MSU	29	39	—	—	68
Connecticut	46	38	—	—	84

VISITORS Connecticut   **Date** Jan. 2, 1990   **Site** Alumni Hall, Jamaica, NY

No.	Player Name		Total FG		3-point		FT	FTA	Rebounds			PF	TP	A	TO	BLK	S	MIN
			FG	FGA	FG	FGA			Off	Def	Tot							
40	Nadav Henefeld	f	1	7	0	5	0	1	3	2	5	2	2	1	2	0	5	34
24	Scott Burrell	f	1	6	0	2	0	0	1	1	2	3	2	1	2	0	0	18
22	Rod Sellers	c	5	10	0	0	1	2	5	0	5	0	11	0	2	1	0	28
13	Chris Smith	g	3	14	1	5	3	4	2	1	3	3	10	1	2	0	4	32
32	Tate George	g	6	12	0	1	0	1	1	3	4	3	12	3	3	0	2	28
20	Murray Williams		3	7	1	1	2	2	1	4	5	2	9	0	3	0	0	17
15	John Gwynn		3	11	0	1	0	0	1	0	1	2	6	0	0	0	1	16
55	Dan Cyrulik		2	5	0	0	1	4	3	3	6	2	5	0	1	0	0	11
21	Steve Pikiell		0	2	0	1	0	0	0	1	1	0	0	1	1	0	0	4
23	Lyman DePriest		0	0	0	0	1	2	0	0	0	2	1	0	0	0	0	6
42	Toraino Walker		2	6	0	0	0	0	3	0	3	1	4	0	0	0	0	6
	TEAM REBOUNDS (included in Totals)								2	4	6							
	TOTALS		26	80	2	16	8	16	22	19	41	20	62	7	16	1	12	200

TOTAL FG %:   1st Half 14-41 34.1   2nd Half 15-39 38.5   Game 26-80 32.5   Deadball
3-Pt. FG %:   1st Half 1-10 10.0   2nd Half 1-6 16.7   Game 2-16 12.5   Rebounds 3
FT%:   1st Half 3-4 75.0   2nd Half 5-12 41.6   Game 8-16 50.0

HOME St. John's

No.	Player Name		Total FG		3-point		FT	FTA	Rebounds			PF	TP	A	TO	BLK	S	MIN
			FG	FGA	FG	FGA			Off	Def	Tot							
11	Jayson Williams	f	11	14	1	1	2	4	2	7	9	2	25	0	2	1	0	26
21	Malik Sealy	f	7	10	0	0	5	6	1	4	5	1	19	2	4	1	5	33
41	Robert Werdann	c	5	5	0	0	0	0	0	7	7	1	10	1	2	3	0	28
3	Boo Harvey	g	7	11	3	5	3	4	0	4	4	1	20	10	2	0	2	32
12	Jason Buchanan	g	1	1	0	0	1	2	0	2	2	1	3	4	2	0	2	25
33	Bill Singleton		0	3	0	0	5	6	2	3	5	2	5	2	1	0	2	24
22	Chuck Sproling		2	3	0	0	0	0	0	1	1	4	4	0	2	1	0	14
4	David Cain		1	1	0	0	0	0	0	0	0	2	2	1	2	0	1	7
13	Barry Milhaven		1	2	0	0	0	0	0	1	1	0	2	0	1	0	0	5
5	Darrell Aiken		0	1	0	1	3	6	0	2	2	0	3	0	1	0	0	2
10	Terence Mullin		0	0	0	0	0	1	0	0	0	0	0	0	1	0	1	4
	TEAM REBOUNDS (included in Totals)								3	2	5							
	TOTALS		35	51	4	7	19	29	8	33	41	14	93	20	20	6	13	200

TOTAL FG %:   1st Half 20-29 68.9   2nd Half 15-32 46.9   Game 35-53 66.0   Deadball
3-Pt. FG %:   1st Half 3-5 60.0   2nd Half 1-2 50.0   Game 4-7 57.1   Rebounds 3
FT%:   1st Half 5-9 55.5   2nd Half 14-20 70.0   Game 19-29 65.5

OFFICIALS: John Clougherty, Robert Donato, Ted Valentine
Technical Fouls: None
Attendance 6,008 (Sellout)

SCORE BY PERIODS	1st H.	2nd H.	OT	OT	FINAL
Connecticut	32	30	—	—	62
St. John's	48	45	—	—	93

VISITORS Pittsburgh **Date** Jan. 6, 1990 **Site** Hartford CC, Hartford, CT

No.	Player Name		Total FG FG	Total FG FGA	3-point FG	3-point FGA	FT	FTA	Rebounds Off	Rebounds Def	Rebounds Tot	PF	TP	A	TO	BLK	S	MIN
00	Brian Shorter	f	4	7	0	0	6	11	2	9	11	4	14	0	3	1	1	34
21	Rod Brookin	f	2	5	1	2	5	6	2	1	3	4	10	0	3	0	1	26
55	Bobby Martin	c	5	10	0	1	5	10	5	7	12	3	15	1	5	1	1	37
20	Darelle Porter	g	1	4	1	2	3	4	1	2	3	5	6	2	7	0	4	36
22	Jason Matthews	g	4	10	1	4	7	7	1	4	5	5	16	1	3	0	0	31
25	John Rasp		0	0	0	0	0	0	0	0	0	0	0	0	3	0	0	3
12	Pat Cavanaugh		0	4	0	3	0	1	0	2	2	1	0	1	1	0	0	14
33	Darren Morningstar		0	0	0	0	0	0	0	2	2	2	0	1	0	0	0	8
42	Gilbert Johnson		0	1	0	0	0	0	0	0	0	0	0	0	0	0	0	5
24	Derrick Layton		0	0	0	0	0	0	0	0	0	0	0	0	0	0	0	1
23	Travis Ziegler		0	1	0	1	0	0	0	0	0	1	0	1	0	0	0	3
15	Brian Brush		0	2	0	0	0	0	0	0	0	1	0	0	1	0	0	2
	TEAM REBOUNDS (included in Totals)								3	2	5							
	TOTALS		16	44	3	13	26	39	14	29	43	26	61	7	26	2	7	200

TOTAL FG %: 1st Half 7-17 41.2 2nd Half 9-27 33.3 Game 16-44 38.4 Deadball
3-Pt. FG %: 1st Half 1-3 33.3 2nd Half 2-10 20.0 Game 3-13 23.1 Rebounds 4
FT%: 1st Half 9-13 69.2 2nd Half 17-26 65.4 Game 26-39 66.7

HOME Connecticut

No.	Player Name		Total FG FG	Total FG FGA	3-point FG	3-point FGA	FT	FTA	Rebounds Off	Rebounds Def	Rebounds Tot	PF	TP	A	TO	BLK	S	MIN
22	Rod Sellers	f	4	8	0	0	0	3	4	2	6	5	8	0	4	6	1	22
40	Nadav Henefeld	f	3	6	0	2	3	4	1	4	5	5	9	4	1	0	5	32
55	Dan Cyrulik	c	0	4	0	0	0	0	3	0	3	4	0	0	1	0	0	18
13	Chris Smith	g	9	18	5	12	5	7	0	1	1	4	28	4	3	0	3	33
32	Tate George	g	6	12	0	2	4	7	4	3	7	3	16	6	2	0	5	35
23	Lyman DePriest		0	3	0	0	0	0	1	5	6	5	0	0	1	1	3	25
15	John Gwynn		1	7	1	2	7	10	0	2	2	1	10	0	4	0	0	11
20	Murray Williams		1	4	0	0	4	4	2	3	5	5	6	3	0	1	0	19
42	Toraino Walker		1	1	0	0	0	0	0	0	0	1	2	0	0	1	0	3
21	Steve Pikiell		0	0	0	0	0	0	0	0	0	0	0	1	0	0	0	1
11	Oliver Macklin		0	0	0	0	0	0	0	0	0	0	0	0	0	0	0	1
	TEAM REBOUNDS (included in Totals)								1	3	4							
	TOTALS		25	63	6	18	23	35	16	23	39	33	79	18	16	9	17	200

TOTAL FG %: 1st Half 12-38 31.6 2nd Half 13-25 52.8 Game 25-63 39.7 Deadball
3-Pt. FG %: 1st Half 3-12 25.0 2nd Half 3-6 50.0 Game 6-18 33.3 Rebounds 5
FT%: 1st Half 3-7 42.9 2nd Half 20-28 71.4 Game 23-35 65.7

OFFICIALS: Jim Burr, Tom Scott, Roger Parramore
Technical Fouls: Pittsburgh Bench
Attendance 16,294 (Sellout)

SCORE BY PERIODS	1st H.	2nd H.	OT	OT	FINAL
Pittsburgh	24	37	—	—	61
Connecticut	30	49	—	—	79

VISITORS Connecticut   **Date** Jan. 9, 1990   **Site** duPont Pavilion, Villanova, PA

No.	Player Name		Total FG FG	Total FG FGA	3-point FG	3-point FGA	FT	FTA	Rebounds Off	Rebounds Def	Rebounds Tot	PF	TP	A	TO	BLK	S	MIN
20	Murray Williams	f	2	7	0	0	0	0	2	2	4	2	4	3	1	0	2	23
40	Nadav Henefeld	f	6	12	0	2	7	9	5	3	8	3	19	3	5	0	6	35
22	Rod Sellers	c	6	10	0	0	6	10	3	4	7	4	18	2	1	1	3	31
13	Chris Smith	g	5	13	4	6	5	6	3	0	0	2	19	2	1	0	0	36
32	Tate George	g	1	5	0	1	2	3	0	1	1	5	4	4	3	1	3	29
55	Dan Cyrulik		0	0	0	0	1	2	0	2	2	1	1	0	1	0	2	3
15	John Gwynn		0	3	0	0	0	0	0	0	0	2	0	0	1	0	0	6
23	Lyman DePriest		2	3	0	0	0	1	1	3	4	1	4	1	1	0	0	19
42	Toraino Walker		1	2	0	0	0	0	1	1	2	1	2	0	0	1	0	7
21	Steve Pikiell		0	0	0	0	0	0	0	1	1	0	0	1	0	0	1	9
11	Oliver Macklin		0	0	0	0	0	0	0	0	0	0	0	0	0	0	0	1
31	Tim Pikiell		0	0	0	0	0	0	0	1	1	0	0	1	1	0	0	1
	TEAM REBOUNDS (included in Totals)								4	2	6							
	TOTALS		23	55	4	9	21	31	19	20	36	21	71	17	15	3	17	200

TOTAL FG %: 1st Half 11-28 39.3   2nd Half 12-27 44.4   Game 23-55 41.8   Deadball
3-Pt. FG %: 1st Half 1-4 25.0   2nd Half 3-5 60.0   Game 4-9 44.4   Rebounds 1
FT%: 1st Half 6-10 60.0   2nd Half 15-21 71.4   Game 21-31 67.7

HOME Villanova

No.	Player Name		Total FG FG	Total FG FGA	3-point FG	3-point FGA	FT	FTA	Rebounds Off	Rebounds Def	Rebounds Tot	PF	TP	A	TO	BLK	S	MIN
14	Lance Miller	f	1	4	1	1	2	2	1	3	4	2	5	1	6	2	0	25
32	Marc Dowdell	f	1	1	0	0	1	2	1	3	4	2	3	1	5	0	3	24
33	Tom Greis	c	4	8	0	0	1	2	4	5	9	1	9	1	3	2	0	21
15	Chris Walker	g	2	5	2	4	0	0	0	1	1	5	6	2	2	0	1	27
24	Greg Woodard	g	1	4	0	1	5	6	1	2	3	2	7	2	1	1	0	25
36	Rodney Taylor		1	2	0	0	2	2	0	1	1	2	4	0	2	1	0	20
21	Calvin Byrd		1	1	0	0	1	3	1	0	1	2	3	1	1	0	0	12
44	Arron Bain		1	6	0	0	0	0	1	0	1	0	2	1	2	0	0	12
12	David Miller		4	5	1	2	2	2	0	2	2	1	11	2	1	0	3	10
20	Bob Tribuiani		1	4	0	2	0	0	1	1	2	2	2	2	0	0	0	6
23	Tim Muller		0	1	0	1	0	0	0	0	0	0	0	0	0	0	0	6
25	Paul Vrind		0	2	0	1	0	0	0	0	0	2	0	0	1	0	0	6
41	James Bryson		1	1	0	0	0	0	0	2	2	4	2	0	1	0	0	6
	TEAM REBOUNDS (included in Totals)								1	4	5							
	TOTALS		18	44	4	12	14	19	11	24	35	25	54	13	25	6	7	200

TOTAL FG %: 1st Half 6-19 31.6   2nd Half 12-25 48.0   Game 18-44 40.9   Deadball
3-Pt. FG %: 1st Half 1-3 33.3   2nd Half 3-9 33.3   Game 4-12 33.3   Rebounds 1
FT%: 1st Half 7-11 63.6   2nd Half 7-8 87.5   Game 14-19 73.7

OFFICIALS: Donnie Gray, Ted Valentine, Frank Scagliotta
Technical Fouls: Conn, Coach Calhoun
Attendance 6,500 (Sellout)

SCORE BY PERIODS	1st H.	2nd H.	OT	OT	FINAL
Connecticut	29	42	—	—	71
Villanova	20	34	—	—	54

VISITORS Connecticut **Date** Jan. 13, 1990 **Site** South Orange, NJ

No.	Player Name		Total FG FG	Total FG FGA	3-point FG	3-point FGA	FT	FTA	Rebounds Off	Rebounds Def	Rebounds Tot	PF	TP	A	TO	BLK	S	MIN
20	Murray Williams	f	2	4	0	0	0	2	0	1	1	2	4	1	2	0	0	16
40	Nadav Henefeld	f	4	7	0	1	6	6	3	5	8	1	14	5	3	0	6	38
22	Rod Sellers	c	8	11	0	0	3	6	4	3	7	2	19	0	2	0	2	34
13	Chris Smith	g	3	6	0	2	2	2	0	1	1	1	8	2	4	0	4	29
32	Tate George	g	4	10	0	0	2	4	0	2	2	3	10	2	2	1	3	32
15	John Gwynn		6	7	2	3	0	0	0	0	0	2	14	0	1	0	2	21
23	Lyman DePriest		2	4	0	0	1	3	1	4	5	2	5	1	0	1	1	22
55	Dan Cyrulik		2	5	0	0	1	2	1	0	1	2	5	0	0	0	0	8
	TEAM REBOUNDS (included in Totals)								2	0	2							
	TOTALS		31	54	2	6	15	25	11	16	27	15	79	11	14	2	18	200

TOTAL FG %: 1st Half 18-34 52.9 2nd Half 13-20 65.0 Game 31-54 57.4 Deadball
3-Pt. FG %: 1st Half 1-4 25.0 2nd Half 1-2 50.0 Game 2-6 33.3 Rebounds 4
FT%: 1st Half 5-7 71.4 2nd Half 10-18 55.6 Game 15-25 60.0

HOME Seton Hall

No.	Player Name		Total FG FG	Total FG FGA	3-point FG	3-point FGA	FT	FTA	Rebounds Off	Rebounds Def	Rebounds Tot	PF	TP	A	TO	BLK	S	MIN
30	Frantz Volcy	f	5	9	0	0	3	4	2	2	4	5	13	1	3	0	1	30
31	Michael Cooper	f	9	12	1	2	2	3	2	0	2	3	21	1	4	1	0	40
32	Anthony Avent	c	5	10	0	0	0	0	4	7	11	3	10	2	6	1	0	37
13	Daryl Crist	g	0	1	0	1	0	0	0	2	2	1	0	2	2	0	0	15
24	Terry Dehere	g	7	12	4	7	0	1	0	3	3	3	18	1	2	0	1	36
20	Oliver Taylor		3	6	2	3	2	2	0	1	1	2	10	2	3	0	1	26
22	Gordon Winchester		2	4	0	0	0	0	1	0	1	3	4	0	1	0	0	10
25	Jim Dickinson		0	0	0	0	0	0	0	1	1	1	0	0	0	0	0	2
33	Marco Lokar		0	0	0	0	0	0	0	0	0	1	0	0	1	0	0	4
	TEAM REBOUNDS (included in Totals)								1	2	3							
	TOTALS		31	54	7	13	7	10	10	18	28	22	76	9	23	2	3	200

TOTAL FG %: 1st Half 12-21 57.1 2nd Half 19-33 57.6 Game 31-54 57.4 Deadball
3-Pt. FG %: 1st Half 5-6 83.3 2nd Half 2-7 28.6 Game 7-13 53.0 Rebounds 0
FT%: 1st Half 2-4 50.0 2nd Half 5-6 83.3 Game 7-10 70.0

OFFICIALS: Gene Monje, Jack Hannon, Joe Kepics
Technical Fouls: None
Attendance 13,621

SCORE BY PERIODS	1st H.	2nd H.	OT	OT	FINAL
Connecticut	42	37	—	—	79
Seton Hall	31	45	—	—	76

VISITORS Syracuse   **Date** Jan. 15, 1990   **Site** Hartford CC, Hartford, CT

No.	Player Name		Total FG FG	Total FG FGA	3-point FG	3-point FGA	FT	FTA	Rebounds Off	Rebounds Def	Rebounds Tot	PF	TP	A	TO	BLK	S	MIN
23	David Johnson	f	2	8	0	0	2	2	2	1	3	3	6	3	0	0	0	28
44	Derrick Coleman	f	5	13	0	0	6	9	2	10	12	1	16	0	2	1	3	37
25	LeRon Ellis	c	7	13	0	0	0	0	9	4	13	4	14	0	1	1	0	32
30	Billy Owens	g	6	19	1	2	0	0	8	3	11	5	13	2	3	0	0	37
32	Stephen Thompson	g	5	12	0	1	0	4	4	2	6	4	10	2	5	0	2	37
12	Michael Edwards		0	5	0	3	0	0	1	0	1	5	0	4	3	0	1	20
34	Richard Manning		0	1	0	0	0	0	0	0	0	0	0	0	0	0	0	9
	TEAM REBOUNDS (included in Totals)								2	1	3							
	TOTALS		25	71	1	6	8	15	28	21	49	22	59	11	14	2	6	200

TOTAL FG %:   1st Half 14-39 41.2   2nd Half 11-37 29.7   Game 25-71 35.2   Deadball
3-Pt. FG %:   1st Half 0-0 00.0   2nd Half 1-6 16.7   Game 1-6 16.7   Rebounds 3
FT%:   1st Half 3-6 50.0   2nd Half 5-9 55.6   Game 8-15 53.3

HOME Connecticut

No.	Player Name		Total FG FG	Total FG FGA	3-point FG	3-point FGA	FT	FTA	Rebounds Off	Rebounds Def	Rebounds Tot	PF	TP	A	TO	BLK	S	MIN
20	Murray Williams	f	1	6	0	0	0	0	1	2	3	1	2	5	2	1	2	21
40	Nadav Henefeld	f	4	8	3	5	0	0	2	5	7	5	11	2	6	0	4	36
22	Rod Sellers	c	3	6	0	0	2	5	3	5	8	4	8	0	3	1	1	36
13	Chris Smith	g	5	9	1	4	6	8	0	1	1	2	17	3	0	0	1	34
32	Tate George	g	5	11	2	3	5	6	3	3	6	1	17	5	3	1	1	34
23	Lyman DePriest		3	5	0	0	3	5	2	3	5	2	9	1	0	0	0	18
55	Dan Cyrulik		1	4	0	0	0	0	2	1	3	0	2	0	1	0	0	8
15	John Gwynn		1	3	0	1	2	2	0	1	1	0	4	2	0	0	1	13
	TEAM REBOUNDS (included in Totals)								1	1	2							
	TOTALS		23	52	6	13	18	26	14	22	36	15	70	18	15	3	10	200

TOTAL FG %:   1st Half 14-29 48.3   2nd Half 9-23 39.1   Game 23-52 44.2   Deadball
3-Pt. FG %:   1st Half 6-9 66.7   2nd Half 0-4 00.0   Game 6-13 46.2   Rebounds 2
FT%:   1st Half 4-5 80.0   2nd Half 14-21 66.7   Game 18-26 69.2

OFFICIALS: Frank Scagliotta, John Clougherty, Larry Lembo
Technical Fouls: SU Bench, UC Bench
Attendance 16,294 (Sellout)

SCORE BY PERIODS	1st H.	2nd H.	OT	OT	FINAL
Syracuse	31	28	—	—	59
Connecticut	38	32	—	—	70

VISITORS Georgetown   **Date** Jan. 20, 1990   **Site** Hartford CC, Hartford, CT

No.	Player Name		Total FG FG	Total FG FGA	3-point FG	3-point FGA	FT	FTA	Rebounds Off	Rebounds Def	Rebounds Tot	PF	TP	A	TO	BLK	S	MIN
33	Alonzo Mourning	f	6	7	0	0	9	10	1	11	12	4	21	0	4	4	0	35
34	Michael Tate	f	0	1	0	1	0	0	0	0	0	1	0	0	0	0	0	8
55	Dikembe Mutombo	c	1	3	0	0	0	1	3	4	7	1	2	1	2	0	0	12
12	Dwayne Bryant	c	4	7	2	5	4	5	1	2	3	3	14	10	2	0	1	39
20	Mark Tillmon	g	8	21	1	8	2	6	1	1	2	5	19	1	5	0	3	33
10	David Edwards		0	1	0	0	0	0	0	0	0	0	0	2	5	0	0	7
30	Ronny Thompson		3	7	1	3	0	0	0	2	2	3	7	1	3	0	0	28
50	Sam Jefferson		1	2	0	0	0	3	6	4	10	3	2	0	1	0	2	32
41	Antoine Stoudamire		0	0	0	0	0	0	0	0	0	1	0	0	0	0	0	5
44	Mike Sabol		0	0	0	0	0	0	0	0	0	1	0	0	0	0	0	1
	TEAM REBOUNDS (included in Totals)								1	2	3							
	TOTALS		23	49	4	17	15	25	13	26	39	22	65	15	22	4	6	200

TOTAL FG %:   1st Half 10-24 41.7   2nd Half 13-26 50.0   Game 23-49 46.9   Deadball
3-Pt. FG %:   1st Half 2-8 25.0   2nd Half 2-9 22.2   Game 4-17 23.5   Rebounds 3
FT%:   1st Half 7-9 77.8   2nd Half 8-16 50.0   Game 15-25 60.0

HOME Connecticut

No.	Player Name		Total FG FG	Total FG FGA	3-point FG	3-point FGA	FT	FTA	Rebounds Off	Rebounds Def	Rebounds Tot	PF	TP	A	TO	BLK	S	MIN
20	Murray Williams	f	0	1	0	0	0	0	1	0	1	3	0	2	1	0	1	18
40	Nadav Henefeld	f	6	12	5	7	4	7	1	4	5	1	21	5	5	0	5	35
22	Rod Sellers	c	1	3	0	0	0	0	2	3	5	5	2	0	0	0	0	25
13	Chris Smith	g	4	12	1	5	2	4	2	5	7	3	11	4	1	0	4	35
32	Tate George	g	4	8	0	0	3	4	0	1	1	1	11	4	1	0	3	33
23	Lyman DePriest		2	3	0	0	2	4	1	4	5	3	6	0	4	0	0	23
15	John Gwynn		5	9	1	1	4	4	0	1	1	2	15	0	1	0	1	15
55	Dan Cyrulik		2	3	0	0	0	0	0	0	0	4	4	1	0	0	0	16
	TEAM REBOUNDS (included in Totals)								1	2	3							
	TOTALS		24	51	7	13	15	23	8	20	28	22	70	16	13	0	14	200

TOTAL FG %:   1st Half 13-27 48.1   2nd Half 11-24 45.8   Game 24-51 47.1   Deadball
3-Pt. FG %:   1st Half 3-7 42.9   2nd Half 4-6 66.7   Game 7-13 53.8   Rebounds 1
FT%:   1st Half 6-11 54.5   2nd Half 9-12 75.0   Game 15-23 65.2

OFFICIALS: Jody Silvester, Joe Minola, Mickey Crowley
Technical Fouls: None
Attendance 16,294 (Sellout)

SCORE BY PERIODS	1st H.	2nd H.	OT	OT	FINAL
Georgetown	29	36	—	—	65
Connecticut	35	35	—	—	70

VISITORS Central Connecticut **Date** Jan. 24, 1990 **Site** Storrs Field House, Storrs, CT

No.	Player Name		Total FG FG	FGA	3-point FG	FGA	FT	FTA	Rebounds Off	Def	Tot	PF	TP	A	TO	BLK	S	MIN
20	Al Williams	f	1	2	0	0	0	0	0	0	0	2	2	0	1	0	0	10
21	Patrick Sellers	f	0	2	0	0	1	4	1	7	8	3	1	4	3	0	1	34
59	Ahmad Ricketts	c	5	7	0	0	5	6	4	1	5	3	15	0	0	0	0	22
22	Kevin Swann	g	6	13	0	1	7	7	1	1	2	1	19	3	3	0	3	37
23	Damian Johnson	g	1	8	0	0	8	8	0	3	3	2	10	0	5	0	2	24
13	Larron Campbell		6	10	0	0	0	0	2	2	4	3	12	2	5	0	2	30
40	Doug Leichner		3	9	0	0	2	2	1	4	5	3	8	1	6	1	2	28
44	David Cargill		0	0	0	0	0	0	0	0	0	0	0	1	0	1	0	2
25	Marc Rybczyk		4	7	2	5	0	0	1	0	1	2	10	1	1	0	0	11
24	Denis Murphy		0	0	0	0	0	0	0	0	0	0	0	0	0	0	1	2
	TEAM REBOUNDS (included in Totals)								4	3	7							
	TOTALS		26	58	2	6	23	27	14	21	35	19	77	12	24	2	11	200

TOTAL FG %: 1st Half 11-28 39.3 2nd Half 15-30 50.0 Game 26-58 44.8 Deadball
3-Pt. FG %: 1st Half 0-0 00.0 2nd Half 2-6 33.3 Game 2-6 33.3 Rebounds 2
FT%: 1st Half 11-12 91.7 2nd Half 12-15 80.0 Game 23-27 85.2

HOME Connecticut

No.	Player Name		Total FG FG	FGA	3- point FG	FGA	FT	FTA	Rebounds Off	Def	Tot	PF	TP	A	TO	BLK	S	MIN
23	Lyman DePriest	f	3	6	0	0	0	2	5	1	6	4	6	0	3	0	1	14
40	Nadav Henefeld	f	5	9	1	4	2	2	3	4	7	2	13	3	3	0	4	23
22	Rod Sellers	c	6	9	0	0	2	2	4	2	6	3	14	1	2	2	0	23
13	Chris Smith	g	6	11	5	8	2	2	1	0	1	4	19	3	2	1	4	26
32	Tate George	g	8	17	0	2	0	1	1	3	4	1	16	5	3	0	2	34
24	Scott Burrell		3	9	1	2	2	2	3	4	7	3	9	6	3	4	3	26
55	Dan Cyrulik		1	2	0	0	1	2	1	0	1	0	3	0	0	0	1	13
15	John Gwynn		5	14	1	3	1	2	2	1	3	3	12	1	1	0	0	21
42	Toraino Walker		3	5	0	0	1	2	2	2	4	1	7	1	1	0	1	16
11	Oliver Macklin		0	0	0	0	0	0	0	0	0	0	0	0	0	0	0	2
30	Marc Suhr		0	2	0	0	0	0	0	0	0	1	0	0	0	0	0	2
	TEAM REBOUNDS (included in Totals)								3	3	6							
	TOTALS		40	84	8	19	11	17	25	20	45	22	99	20	18	7	16	200

TOTAL FG %: 1st Half 19-48 39.6 2nd Half 21-36 58.3 Game 40-84 47.6 Deadball
3-Pt. FG %: 1st Half 4-11 36.4 2nd Half 4-8 50.0 Game 8-19 42.1 Rebounds 4
FT%: 1st Half 5-8 62.5 2nd Half 8-9 66.7 Game 11-17 64.7

OFFICIALS: Bob Madigan, John Cahill, Don Winterton
Technical Fouls: None
Attendance 4,604 (Sellout)

SCORE BY PERIODS	1st H.	2nd H.	OT	OT	FINAL
CCSU	33	44	—	—	77
Connecticut	47	52	—	—	99

VISITORS St. John's **Date** Jan. 27, 1990 **Site** Gampel Pavilion

No.	Player Name		Total FG FG	Total FG FGA	3-point FG	3-point FGA	FT	FTA	Rebounds Off	Rebounds Def	Rebounds Tot	PF	TP	A	TO	BLK	S	MIN
11	Jayson Williams	f	2	7	0	0	2	4	4	3	7	5	6	0	2	1	0	35
21	Malik Sealy	f	10	17	0	0	6	7	4	9	13	5	26	1	1	1	2	39
41	Robert Werdann	c	2	6	0	0	0	0	1	5	6	2	4	0	1	1	0	28
3	Greg Harvey	g	4	7	2	4	0	1	0	3	3	1	10	5	3	0	0	35
12	Jason Buchanan	g	1	6	0	1	0	1	1	3	4	3	2	4	5	0	1	26
33	Billy Singleton		0	7	0	1	0	0	2	4	6	4	0	0	3	0	1	16
22	Chucky Sproling		2	6	1	2	3	4	2	2	4	4	8	1	0	0	0	16
50	Sean Muto		1	1	0	0	0	4	2	0	2	1	2	0	0	0	0	2
4	David Cain		0	0	0	0	0	0	0	0	0	1	0	0	1	0	0	2
13	Barry Milhaven		0	1	0	0	0	0	1	0	1	1	0	0	0	0	0	1
	TEAM REBOUNDS (included in Totals)								2	0	2							
	TOTALS		22	58	3	8	11	21	19	29	48	27	58	11	16	3	4	200

TOTAL FG %: 1st Half 14-28 50.0 2nd Half 8-30 26.7 Game 22-58 37.9 Deadball
3-Pt. FG %: 1st Half 2-3 66.7 2nd Half 1-5 20.0 Game 3-8 37.5 Rebounds 3
FT%: 1st Half 4-6 66.7 2nd Half 7-15 46.7 Game 11-21 52.4

HOME Connecticut

No.	Player Name		Total FG FG	Total FG FGA	3-point FG	3-point FGA	FT	FTA	Rebounds Off	Rebounds Def	Rebounds Tot	PF	TP	A	TO	BLK	S	MIN
23	Lyman DePriest	f	1	1	0	0	0	1	2	2	4	0	2	1	1	0	0	20
40	Nadav Henefeld	f	1	7	0	4	2	5	2	3	5	5	4	5	4	3	4	33
22	Rod Sellers	c	1	5	0	0	0	0	2	1	3	0	2	0	1	1	1	19
13	Chris Smith	g	5	10	3	4	7	8	0	2	2	3	20	3	1	0	1	34
32	Tate George	g	1	10	0	0	4	6	2	5	7	4	6	3	0	0	2	22
24	Scott Burrell		5	7	0	1	2	8	1	3	4	4	12	1	2	0	0	24
15	John Gwynn		6	12	0	1	1	2	1	0	1	1	13	1	0	0	0	24
55	Dan Cyrulik		4	7	0	0	5	6	3	7	10	3	13	1	0	0	1	20
11	Oliver Macklin		0	0	0	0	0	0	0	0	0	0	0	0	0	0	0	1
31	Tim Pikiell		0	1	0	0	0	0	0	0	0	0	0	0	0	0	0	1
30	Marc Suhr		0	0	0	0	0	0	0	0	0	0	0	0	0	0	0	1
42	Toraino Walker		0	0	0	0	0	0	0	0	0	0	0	0	0	0	0	1
	TEAM REBOUNDS (included in Totals)								5	2	7							
	TOTALS		24	60	3	10	21	36	18	25	43	20	72	15	9	4	10	200

TOTAL FG %: 1st Half 13-31 41.9 2nd Half 11-29 37.9 Game 24-60 40.0 Deadball
3-Pt. FG %: 1st Half 3-8 37.5 2nd Half 0-2 00.0 Game 3-10 30.0 Rebounds 3
FT%: 1st Half 6-11 54.5 2nd Half 15-25 60.0 Game 21-36 58.3

OFFICIALS: Larry Lembo, Ted Valentine, Tom Cobin
Technical Fouls: SJ Team
Attendance 8,241 (Sellout)

SCORE BY PERIODS	1st H.	2nd H.	OT	OT	FINAL
St. John's	34	24	—	—	58
Connecticut	35	37	—	—	72

VISITORS Connecticut **Date** Jan. 30, 1990 **Site** Amherst, MA

No.	Player Name		FG	FGA	FG	FGA	FT	FTA	Off	Def	Tot	PF	TP	A	TO	BLK	S	MIN
			Total FG		3-point				Rebounds									
23	Lyman DePriest	f	2	2	0	0	0	0	1	0	1	1	4	0	0	2	3	15
40	Nadav Henefeld	f	3	7	2	4	3	4	1	4	5	3	11	3	2	0	4	29
22	Rod Sellers	c	2	6	0	0	1	2	2	0	2	4	5	1	6	0	0	23
13	Chris Smith	g	8	13	2	3	4	7	1	0	1	2	22	1	2	0	1	38
32	Tate George	g	7	10	0	1	2	3	4	4	8	2	16	12	2	0	2	33
20	Murray Williams		3	4	0	0	3	3	1	1	2	2	9	1	0	1	1	24
15	John Gwynn		5	8	0	0	1	2	1	0	1	1	11	2	0	0	1	10
55	Dan Cyrulik		1	4	0	0	0	1	2	0	2	3	2	0	0	0	0	8
24	Scott Burrell		5	7	1	2	3	5	2	2	4	4	14	2	0	2	1	20
21	Steve Pikiell		0	0	0	0	0	0	0	0	0	0	0	0	0	0	0	0
30	Marc Suhr		0	0	0	0	0	0	0	0	0	0	0	0	0	0	0	0
34	Marte Smith		0	0	0	0	0	0	0	0	0	0	0	0	0	0	0	0
42	Toraino Walker		0	0	0	0	0	0	0	0	0	0	0	0	0	0	0	0
	TEAM REBOUNDS (included in Totals)								0	0	4							
	TOTALS		36	61	5	10	17	27	15	11	30	22	94	22	12	5	13	200

TOTAL FG %: 1st Half 15-30 50.0 2nd Half 21-31 67.7 Game 36-61 59.0 Deadball
3-Pt. FG %: 1st Half 2-5 40.0 2nd Half 3-5 60.0 Game 5-10 50.0 Rebounds 3
FT%: 1st Half 5-8 62.5 2nd Half 12-19 63.4 Game 17-27 62.9

HOME Massachusetts

No.	Player Name		FG	FGA	FG	FGA	FT	FTA	Off	Def	Tot	PF	TP	A	TO	BLK	S	MIN
			Total FG		3-point				Rebounds									
22	Tony Barbee	f	5	9	3	5	2	3	0	4	4	5	15	1	1	0	0	29
31	Harper Williams	f	5	8	0	0	8	8	5	3	8	3	18	0	3	0	0	26
44	John Tate	c	1	4	0	0	2	2	1	2	3	5	4	0	1	0	0	29
14	Cary Herer	g	2	2	0	0	0	0	2	0	2	3	4	11	4	1	2	35
20	Jim McCoy	g	7	16	1	2	7	8	1	3	4	3	22	1	6	0	2	39
34	William Herndon		5	7	0	0	2	3	2	2	4	4	12	3	3	0	0	21
10	Rafer Giles		0	2	0	2	0	0	0	0	0	2	0	0	0	0	0	7
11	Anton Brown		0	1	0	0	0	0	0	0	0	0	0	1	0	0	0	5
35	Tommy Pace		0	1	0	0	0	0	0	0	0	0	0	0	0	1	0	8
12	Chris Bailey		0	0	0	0	0	0	0	0	0	0	0	0	0	0	0	1
	TEAM REBOUNDS (included in Totals)								0	0	3							
	TOTALS		25	50	4	9	21	24	11	14	28	25	75	17	18	2	4	200

TOTAL FG %: 1st Half 13-28 46.4 2nd Half 12-22 54.5 Game 25-50 50.0 Deadball
3-Pt. FG %: 1st Half 1-3 33.3 2nd Half 3-6 50.0 Game 4-9 44.4 Rebounds 2
FT%: 1st Half 6-8 75.0 2nd Half 15-16 93.8 Game 21-24 87.5

OFFICIALS: Larry Lembo, Gerry Donaghy, Bob Donato
Technical Fouls: None
Attendance 4,024 (Capacity)

SCORE BY PERIODS	1st H.	2nd H.	OT	OT	FINAL
Massachusetts	33	42	—	—	75
Connecticut	37	57	—	—	94

VISITORS Connecticut · **Date** Feb. 3, 1990 · **Site** Providence CC, Providence, RI

No.	Player Name		Total FG FG	FGA	3-point FG	FGA	FT	FTA	Rebounds Off	Def	Tot	PF	TP	A	TO	BLK	S	MIN
20	Murray Williams	f	0	4	0	0	6	7	0	0	0	1	6	1	1	0	3	17
40	Nadav Henefeld	f	4	12	0	4	4	4	2	6	8	3	12	3	1	0	0	35
22	Rod Sellers	c	3	7	0	0	6	8	5	3	8	4	12	1	2	0	0	28
13	Chris Smith	g	7	16	1	3	6	11	2	3	5	3	24	2	3	0	1	33
32	Tate George	g	3	7	0	0	7	9	2	3	5	3	13	2	1	0	2	31
24	Scott Burrell		1	2	0	1	3	4	1	1	2	5	5	0	0	1	1	12
23	Lyman DePriest		3	3	0	0	0	0	1	0	1	0	6	0	0	0	2	10
15	John Gwynn		5	10	1	3	4	5	2	1	3	2	15	1	3	0	0	18
55	Dan Cyrulik		0	0	0	0	0	0	2	1	3	4	0	1	1	0	0	10
42	Toraino Walker		0	0	0	0	2	3	0	3	3	1	2	1	0	0	0	5
11	Oliver Macklin		0	0	0	0	0	0	0	0	0	0	0	0	0	0	0	1
	TEAM REBOUNDS (included in Totals)								0	2	2							
	TOTALS		26	61	2	11	38	51	17	23	40	26	92	12	12	1	9	200

TOTAL FG %: 1st Half 16-34 47.1 · 2nd Half 10-27 37.0 · Game 26-61 42.6
3-Pt. FG %: 1st Half 0-6 0.00 · 2nd Half 2-5 40.0 · Game 2-11 18.2
FT%: 1st Half 14-21 66.7 · 2nd Half 24-30 80.0 · Game 38-51 74.5
Deadball Rebounds 7

HOME Providence

No.	Player Name		Total FG FG	FGA	3-point FG	FGA	FT	FTA	Rebounds Off	Def	Tot	PF	TP	A	TO	BLK	S	MIN
15	Quinton Burton	f	5	14	0	4	3	4	4	6	10	6	13	1	3	0	0	34
30	Marty Conlon	f	3	7	1	3	4	7	3	5	8	5	11	6	4	0	0	36
25	Abdul Shamsid-Deen	c	3	7	0	0	0	1	2	2	4	1	6	0	2	1	0	25
14	Eric Murdock	g	6	10	2	5	0	1	0	1	1	5	14	3	3	4	2	28
33	Chris Watts	g	2	3	1	2	0	0	0	1	1	5	5	0	0	0	1	15
24	Marques Bragg		1	3	0	0	0	2	2	0	2	2	2	0	2	1	0	12
11	Carlton Screen		5	10	3	5	4	4	0	2	2	2	17	7	2	0	0	33
55	Marvin Saddler		0	0	0	0	0	0	0	1	1	2	0	0	1	0	0	2
32	Tony Turner		2	5	1	3	1	2	0	1	1	2	6	0	1	0	0	8
23	Greg Bent		0	0	0	0	0	0	0	0	0	0	0	0	0	0	0	2
20	Trent Forbes		1	1	1	1	0	0	0	1	1	1	3	3	2	0	2	5
	TEAM REBOUNDS (included in Totals)								3	4	7							
	TOTALS		28	60	9	23	12	21	14	24	38	31	77	20	20	6	5	200

TOTAL FG %: 1st Half 10-24 41.7 · 2nd Half 18-36 50.0 · Game 28-60 46.7
3-Pt. FG %: 1st Half 3-9 33.3 · 2nd Half 6-14 42.9 · Game 9-22 39.1
FT%: 1st Half 5-9 55.6 · 2nd Half 7-12 58.3 · Game 12-21 57.1
Deadball Rebounds 4

OFFICIALS: Jackie Hannon, Dan Chrisman, Joe Mingle
Technical Fouls: None
Attendance 13,160

SCORE BY PERIODS	1st H.	2nd H.	OT	OT	FINAL
Connecticut	46	46	—	—	92
Providence	28	49	—	—	77

VISITORS Fairfield (7-12) **Date** Feb. 6, 1990 **Site** Gampel Pavilion, Storrs, CT

No.	Player Name		Total FG FG	Total FG FGA	3-point FG	3-point FGA	FT	FTA	Rebounds Off	Rebounds Def	Rebounds Tot	PF	TP	A	TO	BLK	S	MIN
20	Ed Duncan	f	6	8	0	0	3	4	1	3	4	1	15	0	3	0	0	36
22	Drew Henderson	f	1	7	0	0	2	4	5	7	12	2	4	0	7	1	1	36
50	Harold Brantley	c	0	5	0	0	1	4	2	0	2	2	1	1	5	2	1	33
15	Marvin Walters	g	4	12	0	4	2	3	1	3	4	5	10	4	7	0	0	31
24	Kevin George	g	2	4	0	0	0	0	0	3	3	1	4	2	1	0	0	37
14	Greg Keith		0	0	0	0	0	0	0	2	2	3	0	0	1	0	0	9
44	Mike Rodgers		1	2	0	0	0	0	0	1	1	0	2	0	0	0	2	14
34	Ed Newman		0	0	0	0	0	0	0	0	0	0	0	0	0	0	0	2
54	Mike Plansky		1	1	1	1	0	0	0	0	0	0	3	1	0	0	0	2
	TEAM REBOUNDS (included in Totals)								1	2	3							
	TOTALS		15	39	1	5	8	15	10	21	31	14	39	8	24	3	4	200

TOTAL FG %: 1st Half 10-19 52.6 2nd Half 5-20 25.0 Game 15-39 38.5 Deadball
3-Pt. FG %: 1st Half 0-1 0.0 2nd Half 1-4 25.0 Game 1-5 20.0 Rebounds 4
FT%: 1st Half 3-3 100.0 2nd Half 5-12 41.7 Game 8-15 53.3

HOME Connecticut (20-3)

No.	Player Name		Total FG FG	Total FG FGA	3-point FG	3-point FGA	FT	FTA	Rebounds Off	Rebounds Def	Rebounds Tot	PF	TP	A	TO	BLK	S	MIN
20	Murray Williams	f	1	4	0	0	1	1	2	1	3	1	3	2	2	0	2	17
40	Nadav Henefeld	f	8	12	2	4	0	0	2	3	5	3	18	5	0	0	3	28
22	Rod Sellers	c	3	6	0	0	0	0	3	3	6	2	6	0	2	2	1	22
13	Chris Smith	g	3	11	2	4	2	2	1	0	1	1	10	2	0	0	1	30
32	Tate George	g	5	10	1	3	2	2	3	4	7	2	13	3	2	0	2	28
23	Lyman DePriest		3	4	0	0	0	1	0	0	0	1	6	0	0	0	2	11
24	Scott Burrell		1	4	0	0	0	0	1	1	2	3	2	0	2	0	3	22
42	Toraino Walker		1	3	0	0	0	0	2	2	4	2	2	0	0	1	0	16
15	John Gwynn		4	11	0	0	1	2	3	0	3	1	9	1	0	0	0	19
55	Dan Cyrulik		0	0	0	0	0	2	0	0	0	0	0	0	1	0	1	2
21	Steve Pikiell		1	2	1	1	0	0	1	0	1	0	3	0	0	0	0	3
11	Oliver Macklin		1	1	0	0	0	0	0	1	1	0	2	0	0	0	0	2
	TEAM REBOUNDS (included in Totals)								2	1	3							
	TOTALS		31	68	6	12	6	10	20	16	36	16	74	13	9	3	15	200

TOTAL FG %: 1st Half 12-33 36.4 2nd Half 19-35 54.3 Game 31-68 45.6 Deadball
3-Pt. FG %: 1st Half 1-4 25.0 2nd Half 5-8 62.5 Game 6-12 50.0 Rebounds 1
FT%: 1st Half 3-5 60.0 2nd Half 3-5 60.0 Game 6-10 60.0

OFFICIALS: Joe Mingle, Bob Madigan, John Cahill
Technical Fouls: None
Attendance 8,148 (Sellout)

SCORE BY PERIODS	1st H.	2nd H.	OT	OT	FINAL
Fairfield	23	16	—	—	39
Connecticut	28	46	—	—	74

VISITORS Connecticut (20-4) **Date** Feb. 10, 1990 **Site** Carrier Dome, Syracuse, NY

No.	Player Name		Total FG FG	Total FG FGA	3-point FG	3-point FGA	FT	FTA	Rebounds Off	Rebounds Def	Rebounds Tot	PF	TP	A	TO	BLK	S	MIN
40	Nadav Henefeld	f	5	13	3	7	0	0	1	3	4	3	13	5	3	0	2	37
20	Murray Williams	f	0	2	0	0	0	0	1	0	1	0	0	1	2	0	1	5
22	Rod Sellers	c	1	2	0	0	0	0	4	0	4	5	2	0	1	0	0	21
32	Tate George	g	6	8	1	1	2	4	2	1	3	3	15	4	0	1	1	25
13	Chris Smith	g	9	20	3	9	4	4	6	2	8	2	25	4	2	0	1	37
23	Lyman DePriest		3	4	0	0	0	2	3	0	3	5	6	1	2	0	0	8
55	Dan Cyrulik		0	4	0	0	0	0	1	3	4	4	0	1	1	1	0	13
42	Toraino Walker		0	1	0	0	0	0	1	1	2	1	0	0	1	0	0	6
15	John Gwynn		4	10	3	5	4	4	3	1	4	0	15	0	1	0	0	22
24	Scott Burrell		4	8	2	6	0	1	0	3	3	5	10	2	2	1	1	26
	TEAM REBOUNDS (included in Totals)								1	4	5							
	TOTALS		32	72	12	28	10	15	23	18	41	28	86	18	15	3	6	200

TOTAL FG %: 1st Half 11-33 33.3 2nd Half 21-39 53.8 Game 32-72 44.4 Deadball
3-Pt. FG %: 1st Half 6-14 42.9 2nd Half 6-14 42.9 Game 12-28 42.9 Rebounds 2
FT%: 1st Half 3-4 75.0 2nd Half 7-11 63.6 Game 10-15 66.7

HOME Syracuse (18-3)

No.	Player Name		Total FG FG	Total FG FGA	3-point FG	3-point FGA	FT	FTA	Rebounds Off	Rebounds Def	Rebounds Tot	PF	TP	A	TO	BLK	S	MIN
44	Derrick Coleman	f	8	13	1	1	12	13	5	7	12	3	29	3	4	1	0	37
32	Stephen Thompson	f	6	11	1	2	6	8	0	4	4	2	19	6	1	1	0	39
35	LeRon Ellis	c	5	10	0	1	4	6	2	4	6	3	14	3	1	4	4	34
30	Billy Owens	g	8	12	2	3	3	6	3	3	6	2	21	4	1	1	3	36
12	Michael Edwards	g	1	3	1	2	0	0	0	0	0	5	3	7	5	0	1	29
34	Rich Manning		2	3	0	0	0	0	2	1	3	0	4	0	0	1	0	9
4	Dave Johnson		0	1	0	1	0	0	0	1	1	2	0	1	0	0	0	5
40	Tony Scott		0	1	0	1	0	0	0	0	0	2	0	0	0	0	0	11
	TEAM REBOUNDS (included in Totals)								2	0	2							
	TOTALS		30	54	5	11	25	33	14	20	34	19	90	24	12	8	8	200

TOTAL FG %: 1st Half 18-31 58.1 2nd Half 12-23 52.2 Game 30-54 55.6 Deadball
3-Pt. FG %: 1st Half 5-9 55.6 2nd Half 0-2 0.0 Game 5-11 45.5 Rebounds 0
FT%: 1st Half 2-3 66.7 2nd Half 23-30 76.7 Game 25-33 75.8

OFFICIALS: Jim Howell, Jack Hannon, Tom Corbin
Technical Fouls: Connecticut (Burrell)
Attendance 32,820 (Sellout)

SCORE BY PERIODS	1st H.	2nd H.	OT	OT	FINAL
Connecticut	31	55	—	—	86
Syracuse	43	47	—	—	90

VISITORS Connecticut **Date** Feb. 13, 1990 **Site** Fitzgerald Field House, Pittsburgh, PA

No.	Player Name		Total FG		3-point		FT	FTA	Rebounds			PF	TP	A	TO	BLK	S	MIN
			FG	FGA	FG	FGA			Off	Def	Tot							
23	Lyman DePriest	f	3	4	0	0	0	0	2	3	5	5	6	1	4	0	2	19
40	Nadav Henefeld	f	9	17	2	6	7	7	2	3	5	4	27	4	4	0	4	39
22	Rod Sellers	c	4	7	0	0	0	4	1	5	6	5	8	1	2	2	0	26
13	Chris Smith	g	6	9	4	5	6	8	0	2	2	2	22	2	0	0	1	39
32	Tate George	g	0	4	0	2	2	2	1	0	1	4	2	6	2	0	2	27
24	Scott Burrell		3	4	0	0	3	4	0	3	3	0	9	3	3	1	0	24
15	John Gwynn		3	7	0	0	0	0	2	0	2	1	6	0	1	0	0	15
55	Dan Cyrulik		0	1	0	0	0	0	0	0	0	0	0	0	0	0	0	6
20	Murray Williams		0	0	0	0	0	0	0	0	0	0	0	0	1	0	0	1
42	Toraino Walker		0	0	0	0	0	0	0	0	0	2	0	1	1	0	1	4
	TEAM REBOUNDS (included in Totals)								0	5	5							
	TOTALS		28	53	6	13	18	25	8	21	29	23	80	18	18	3	10	200

TOTAL FG %: 1st Half 12-26 46.2   2nd Half 16-27 59.3   Game 28-53 52.8   Deadball
3-Pt. FG %: 1st Half 4-9 44.4   2nd Half 2-4 50.0   Game 6-13 46.2   Rebounds 3
FT%: 1st Half 10-14 71.4   2nd Half 8-11 72.7   Game 18-25 72.0

HOME Pittsburgh

No.	Player Name		Total FG		3-point		FT	FTA	Rebounds			PF	TP	A	TO	BLK	S	MIN
			FG	FGA	FG	FGA			Off	Def	Tot							
00	Brian Shorter	f	9	13	0	0	9	12	4	10	14	4	27	1	3	0	2	40
55	Bobby Martin	f	4	7	0	0	2	3	2	3	5	4	10	1	3	0	0	36
33	Darren Morningstar	c	1	1	0	0	1	1	0	1	1	2	3	0	1	0	0	8
20	Darelle Porter	g	4	9	0	1	2	2	2	1	3	5	10	11	7	0	2	40
22	Jason Matthews	g	3	9	1	3	2	2	0	2	2	2	9	1	3	0	0	36
21	Rod Brookin		5	13	3	5	1	2	0	3	3	3	14	1	3	1	1	33
12	Pat Cavanaugh		1	2	0	0	2	2	0	0	0	1	4	1	0	0	0	7
	TEAM REBOUNDS (included in Totals)								0	1	1							
	TOTALS		27	54	4	9	19	24	8	21	29	21	77	16	20	1	5	200

TOTAL FG %: 1st Half 13-26 50.0   2nd Half 14-28 50.0   Game 27-54 50.0   Deadball
3-Pt. FG %: 1st Half 3-6 50.0   2nd Half 1-3 33.3   Game 4-9 44.4   Rebounds 3
FT%: 1st Half 6-8 75.0   2nd Half 13-16 81.3   Game 19-24 79.2

OFFICIALS: Jim Burr, Ted Valentine, Dan Chrisman
Technical Fouls: Evans (2), Calhoun
Attendance 6,798 (Sellout)

SCORE BY PERIODS	1st H.	2nd H.	OT	OT	FINAL
Connecticut	38	42	—	—	80
Pittsburgh	35	42	—	—	77

VISITORS Boston College   **Date** Feb. 17, 1990   **Site** Gampel Pavilion, Storrs, CT

No.	Player Name		Total FG		3-point		FT	FTA	Rebounds			PF	TP	A	TO	BLK	S	MIN
			FG	FGA	FG	FGA			Off	Def	Tot							
23	Michael Reese	f	2	6	0	0	0	1	1	3	4	4	4	3	1	0	0	27
35	Doug Able	f	6	14	0	0	3	4	5	4	9	5	15	1	5	1	2	35
44	David Hinton	c	5	10	0	1	5	6	1	5	6	4	15	1	3	0	0	26
14	Lior Arditti	g	5	7	5	6	5	7	1	0	1	5	20	4	4	0	5	31
15	Bryan Edwards	g	1	8	0	3	1	2	0	4	4	5	3	1	4	0	1	32
22	Corey Jackson		0	1	0	0	0	2	1	1	2	0	0	1	0	0	0	8
30	Bobby Moran		1	4	0	2	0	0	0	0	0	2	2	1	4	0	0	12
31	Corey Beasley		3	3	0	0	0	2	2	1	3	4	6	0	0	0	0	13
40	Reggie Pruitt		0	0	0	0	0	0	0	1	1	1	0	0	0	0	0	6
11	Bobby Ray Smith		0	1	0	0	0	0	0	0	0	1	0	0	2	0	1	2
32	Walter Lundy		1	2	0	1	0	1	0	0	0	2	2	1	0	0	0	6
50	Willy Foley		0	0	0	0	0	0	0	0	0	0	0	0	0	0	0	1
55	Daryl Michals		0	0	0	0	0	0	0	0	0	0	0	0	0	0	0	1
	TEAM REBOUNDS (included in Totals)								2	2	4							
	TOTALS		24	56	5	13	14	25	13	21	34	33	67	13	23	1	9	200

TOTAL FG %: 1st Half 12-27 44.4   2nd Half 12-29 41.4   Game 24-56 42.9   Deadball
3-Pt. FG %: 1st Half 1-2 50.0   2nd Half 4-11 36.4   Game 5-13 38.5   Rebounds 3
FT%:   1st Half 7-12 58.3   2nd Half 7-13 53.8   Game 14-25 56.0

HOME Connecticut

No.	Player Name		Total FG		3-point		FT	FTA	Rebounds			PF	TP	A	TO	BLK	S	MIN
			FG	FGA	FG	FGA			Off	Def	Tot							
23	Lyman DePriest	f	0	1	0	0	0	0	2	1	3	1	0	0	2	0	0	12
40	Nadav Henefeld	f	5	8	2	2	3	4	2	2	4	4	15	1	3	2	1	26
22	Rod Sellers	c	4	7	0	0	8	9	4	5	9	5	16	0	3	1	0	21
13	Chris Smith	g	4	11	1	4	4	4	2	2	4	1	13	4	1	0	1	37
32	Tate George	g	5	7	2	2	4	6	0	4	4	1	16	6	2	0	2	27
15	John Gwynn		6	8	1	1	5	7	0	0	0	2	18	0	2	0	1	17
55	Dan Cyrulik		1	3	0	0	0	0	0	1	1	3	2	1	0	0	0	10
24	Scott Burrell		1	3	0	0	0	5	2	3	5	3	2	2	4	1	3	23
20	Murray Williams		1	1	0	0	1	3	1	3	4	0	3	3	1	0	3	13
42	Toraino Walker		1	3	0	0	2	6	3	2	5	1	4	1	0	0	0	11
21	Steve Pikiell		0	1	0	0	0	0	0	1	1	0	0	1	0	0	1	2
11	Oliver Macklin		0	0	0	0	0	0	1	0	1	0	0	0	1	0	0	1
	TEAM REBOUNDS (included in Totals)								0	1	1							
	TOTALS		28	53	6	9	27	44	17	25	42	21	89	19	19	4	12	200

TOTAL FG %: 1st Half 13-26 50.0   2nd Half 15-27 55.6   Game 28-53 52.8   Deadball
3-Pt. FG %: 1st Half 4-5 80.0   2nd Half 2-4 50.0   Game 6-9 66.7   Rebounds 6
FT%:   1st Half 13-18 72.7   2nd Half 14-26 53.8   Game 27-44 61.4

OFFICIALS: Mickey Crowley, Jodi Silvester, Bob Donato
Technical Fouls: UC Bench
Attendance 8,302 (Sellout)

SCORE BY PERIODS	1st H.	2nd H.	OT	OT	FINAL
Boston College	32	35	—	—	67
Connecticut	43	46	—	—	89

182

VISITORS Providence **Date** Feb. 19, 1990 **Site** Gampel Pavilion, Storrs, CT

| No. | Player Name | | Total FG | | 3-point | | FT | FTA | Rebounds | | | PF | TP | A | TO | BLK | S | MIN |
			FG	FGA	FG	FGA			Off	Def	Tot							
15	Quinton Burton	f	5	13	2	4	0	2	2	7	9	4	12	1	5	2	0	43
25	Abdul Shamsid-Deen	f	2	4	0	0	1	2	1	4	5	4	5	0	1	1	0	25
50	Marty Conlon	c	3	10	0	3	4	7	4	6	10	4	10	5	5	0	1	42
11	Carlton Screen	g	5	10	0	2	2	4	0	3	3	5	12	5	7	0	2	42
33	Chris Watts	g	2	4	2	4	0	0	0	1	1	2	6	0	0	0	0	15
14	Eric Murdock		5	11	2	5	9	13	3	3	6	5	21	2	2	2	1	34
24	Marques Bragg		3	4	0	0	0	1	1	4	5	2	6	0	2	0	2	20
20	Trent Forbes		0	0	0	0	0	0	0	1	1	0	0	0	0	0	0	1
55	Marvin Saddler		0	0	0	0	0	0	0	0	0	1	0	0	0	0	0	2
23	Greg Bent		0	0	0	0	0	0	0	0	0	0	0	0	0	0	0	1
	TEAM REBOUNDS (included in Totals)								2	5	7							
	TOTALS		25	56	6	18	16	29	13	34	47	27	72	13	22	5	6	225

TOTAL FG %: 1st Half 11-25 44.0   2nd Half 12-27 44.4   OT 2-4 50.0   Game 25-56 44.6
3-Pt. FG %: 1st Half 2-7 28.6   2nd Half 3-8 37.8   OT 1-3 33.3   Game 6-18 33.3
FT%: 1st Half 4-9 44.4   2nd Half 8-12 66.7   OT 4-8 50.0   Game 16-29 55.2
Deadball Rebounds 3

HOME Connecticut

| No. | Player Name | | Total FG | | 3-point | | FT | FTA | Rebounds | | | PF | TP | A | TO | BLK | S | MIN |
			FG	FGA	FG	FGA			Off	Def	Tot							
23	Lyman DePriest	f	0	0	0	0	2	2	3	1	4	5	2	2	0	0	3	12
40	Nadav Henefeld	f	3	9	2	6	2	4	2	7	9	4	10	2	1	0	4	37
22	Rod Sellers	c	2	6	0	0	1	4	2	3	5	2	5	3	0	1	0	32
13	Chris Smith	g	3	11	0	4	11	13	1	2	3	6	17	4	7	0	4	36
32	Tate George	g	7	13	2	5	0	0	1	3	4	4	16	3	2	1	1	39
24	Scott Burrell		5	12	0	2	2	4	2	5	7	4	12	0	0	1	2	31
15	John Gwynn		4	13	0	0	1	3	3	1	4	1	9	0	1	0	0	16
20	Murray Williams		1	1	0	0	0	0	0	0	0	0	2	0	0	0	0	7
55	Dan Cryulik		0	1	0	0	2	2	0	3	3	1	2	0	1	0	0	11
42	Toraino Walker		0	0	0	0	0	0	0	0	0	0	0	2	0	1	0	4
	TEAM REBOUNDS (included in Totals)								2	3	5							
	TOTALS		25	66	4	17	21	32	16	28	44	27	75	16	12	4	14	225

TOTAL FG %: 1st Half 13-33 39.4   2nd Half 8-28 28.6   OT 4-5 80.0   Game 25-66 37.9
3-Pt. FG %: 1st Half 2-9 22.2   2nd Half 1-7 14.3   OT 1-1 100.0   Game 4-17 23.5
FT%: 1st Half 11-12 91.7   2nd Half 7-16 43.8   OT 3-4 75.0   Game 21-32 65.6
Deadball Rebounds 2

OFFICIALS: Gene Monje, John Clougherty, Tom Corbin
Technical Fouls: None
Attendance 8,302 (Sellout)

SCORE BY PERIODS	1st H.	2nd H.	OT	OT	FINAL
Providence	28	35	9	—	72
Connecticut	39	24	12	—	75

VISITORS Seton Hall   **Date** Feb. 24, 1990   **Site** Harry A. Gampel Pavilion, Storrs, CT

No.	Player Name		Total FG FG	Total FG FGA	3-point FG	3-point FGA	FT	FTA	Rebounds Off	Rebounds Def	Rebounds Tot	PF	TP	A	TO	BLK	S	MIN
30	Frantz Volcy	f	4	9	0	0	7	8	6	3	9	5	15	1	1	0	0	32
31	Michael Cooper	f	2	6	0	0	4	5	2	2	4	2	8	1	1	0	1	37
32	Anthony Avent	c	1	6	0	0	4	5	2	3	5	6	6	0	3	2	1	23
24	Terry Dehere	g	4	13	3	10	3	6	3	2	5	2	14	1	6	0	0	35
33	Marco Lokar	g	0	0	0	0	0	0	0	0	0	0	0	0	2	0	1	5
20	Oliver Taylor		3	8	0	3	2	3	0	1	1	2	8	1	3	0	0	21
13	Daryl Crist		1	4	1	4	0	0	0	1	1	3	3	3	4	0	1	21
22	Gordon Winchester		1	1	0	0	1	2	2	2	4	2	3	0	1	0	0	20
25	Jim Dickinson		0	0	0	0	0	0	0	0	0	0	0	0	1	0	0	6
	TEAM REBOUNDS (included in Totals)								3	2	5							
	TOTALS		16	47	4	17	21	29	18	16	34	22	57	7	22	2	4	200

TOTAL FG %:   1st Half 5-22 22.7   2nd Half 11-25 44.0   Game 16-47 34.0   Deadball
3-Pt. FG %:   1st Half 1-8 12.5   2nd Half 3-9 33.3   Game 4-17 23.5   Rebounds 3
FT%:   1st Half 13-19 68.4   2nd Half 8-10 80.0   Game 21-29 72.4

HOME Connecticut

No.	Player Name		Total FG FG	Total FG FGA	3-point FG	3-point FGA	FT	FTA	Rebounds Off	Rebounds Def	Rebounds Tot	PF	TP	A	TO	BLK	S	MIN
23	Lyman DePriest	f	1	4	0	0	0	0	2	2	4	1	2	0	0	0	1	18
40	Nadav Henefeld	f	5	6	1	2	4	4	1	2	3	3	15	5	0	1	6	22
22	Rod Sellers	c	1	2	0	0	1	2	1	2	3	5	3	1	4	2	1	18
13	Chris Smith	g	7	15	1	5	6	7	0	0	0	1	21	3	2	0	2	32
32	Tate George	g	5	8	0	0	3	4	1	2	3	3	13	5	3	0	2	32
55	Dan Cryulik		3	6	0	0	2	3	2	2	4	2	8	0	1	1	0	17
24	Scott Burrell		1	4	0	1	2	3	1	2	3	2	4	1	1	0	3	22
20	Murray Williams		2	2	0	0	0	0	0	2	2	3	4	0	0	0	0	13
15	John Gwynn		1	5	0	1	2	2	0	1	1	1	4	0	0	0	0	14
42	Toraino Walker		1	1	0	0	1	2	0	0	0	1	3	0	0	0	2	9
31	Steve Pikiell		0	0	0	0	2	2	0	0	0	0	2	1	0	0	0	2
11	Oliver Macklin		0	1	0	0	0	0	0	0	0	0	0	0	0	0	0	1
	TEAM REBOUNDS (included in Totals)								5	3	8							
	TOTALS		27	54	2	9	23	29	13	18	31	22	79	16	11	4	17	200

TOTAL FG %:   1st Half 14-26 53.8   2nd Half 13-28 46.4   Game 27-54 50.0   Deadball
3-Pt. FG %:   1st Half 1-4 25.0   2nd Half 1-5 20.0   Game 2-9 22.2   Rebounds 4
FT%:   1st Half 6-8 75.0   2nd Half 17-21 80.9   Game 23-29 79.3

OFFICIALS: Tim Higgins, Joe Mingle, Bob Donato
Technical Fouls: None
Attendance 8,302 (Sellout)

SCORE BY PERIODS	1st H.	2nd H.	OT	OT	FINAL
Seton Hall	24	33	—	—	57
Connecticut	35	44	—	—	79

VISITORS Connecticut   **Date** Feb. 28, 1990   **Site** Capital Centre, Landover, MD

No.	Player Name		Total FG		3-point		FT	FTA	Rebounds			PF	TP	A	TO	BLK	S	MIN
			FG	FGA	FG	FGA			Off	Def	Tot							
23	Lyman DePriest	f	0	1	0	0	0	0	3	1	4	2	0	0	1	0	0	11
40	Nadav Henefeld	f	1	5	1	3	5	6	1	3	4	6	8	2	0	3	3	33
22	Rod Sellers	c	1	3	0	0	4	9	4	2	6	4	6	0	0	0	0	33
13	Chris Smith	g	7	26	2	12	5	6	0	2	2	5	21	1	1	0	2	38
32	Tate George	g	4	13	1	4	1	2	1	2	3	3	10	3	5	0	1	32
24	Scott Burrell		1	5	0	2	2	2	3	1	4	6	4	2	1	1	3	19
20	Murray Williams		1	3	0	0	0	0	1	0	1	2	2	0	0	0	0	7
55	Dan Cyrulik		0	0	0	0	0	0	0	2	2	3	0	0	1	0	0	4
42	Toraino Walker		0	0	0	0	0	0	0	1	1	1	0	0	0	0	0	5
15	John Gwynn		4	11	2	5	3	6	0	1	1	3	13	0	3	0	2	18
	TEAM REBOUNDS (included in Totals)								5	2	7							
	TOTALS		19	67	6	26	20	31	18	17	35	35	64	8	12	4	11	200

TOTAL FG %: 1st Half 8-33 24.2   2nd Half 11-34 32.4   Game 19-67 28.4   Deadball
3-Pt. FG %: 1st Half 3-14 21.4   2nd Half 3-12 25.0   Game 6-26 23.1   Rebounds 5
FT%:   1st Half 9-11 81.8   2nd Half 11-20 55.0   Game 20-31 64.5

HOME Georgetown

No.	Player Name		Total FG		3-point		FT	FTA	Rebounds			PF	TP	A	TO	BLK	S	MIN
			FG	FGA	FG	FGA			Off	Def	Tot							
24	Anthony Allen	f	0	1	0	0	0	0	0	0	0	1	0	0	1	0	1	13
33	Alonzo Mourning	f	5	5	0	0	10	12	5	7	12	6	20	1	2	2	1	28
55	Dikembo Mutombo	c	5	7	0	0	5	8	6	8	14	2	15	1	4	4	1	30
12	Dwayne Bryant	g	5	14	2	4	8	9	1	4	5	2	20	1	6	0	0	35
20	Mark Tillmon	g	3	9	0	3	3	4	2	5	7	3	9	1	4	2	1	27
18	David Edwards		0	2	0	1	6	9	0	1	1	3	6	7	4	0	3	25
30	Ronny Thompson		1	1	1	1	0	0	0	1	1	0	3	0	0	0	0	10
50	Sam Jefferson		3	4	0	0	0	2	0	7	7	5	6	0	4	1	2	20
41	Antoine Stoudamire		1	3	1	3	2	2	1	1	2	1	5	0	0	0	0	11
44	Mike Sabol		0	0	0	0	0	0	0	0	0	0	0	0	0	0	0	1
	TEAM REBOUNDS (included in Totals)								0	1	1							
	TOTALS		23	46	4	12	34	46	15	35	50	23	84	11	25	9	9	200

TOTAL FG %: 1st Half 11-24 45.8   2nd Half 12-22 54.5   Game 23-46 50.0   Deadball
3-Pt. FG %: 1st Half 1-5 20.0   2nd Half 3-7 42.9   Game 4-12 33.3   Rebounds 4
FT%:   1st Half 15-21 71.4   2nd Half 19-25 76.0   Game 34-46 73.9

OFFICIALS: Pete Pavis, Gene Monje, Donnee Gray
Technical Fouls: Calhoun-UC
Attendance 19,035 (Sellout)

SCORE BY PERIODS	1st H.	2nd H.	OT	OT	FINAL
Connecticut	28	36	—	—	64
Georgetown	38	46	—	—	84

VISITORS Connecticut   **Date** March 3, 1990   **Site** Conte Forum, Chestnut Hill, MA

No.	Player Name		FG	FGA	FG	FGA	FT	FTA	Off	Def	Tot	PF	TP	A	TO	BLK	S	MIN
			Total FG		**3-point**				**Rebounds**									
40	Nadav Henefeld	f	5	11	2	4	6	7	1	5	6	3	18	2	1	1	2	30
22	Rod Sellers	f	4	5	0	0	8	10	5	3	8	5	16	0	1	0	0	24
23	Lyman DePriest	c	2	3	0	0	0	0	1	0	1	0	4	0	1	0	1	9
32	Tate George	g	3	8	0	1	6	6	0	2	2	4	12	3	5	1	4	31
13	Chris Smith	g	6	12	0	2	3	3	0	3	3	4	15	3	1	0	0	37
55	Dan Cyrulik		1	1	0	0	2	2	0	0	0	2	4	0	1	0	0	10
15	John Gwynn		3	6	1	1	6	8	0	2	2	3	13	1	2	0	1	19
24	Scott Burrell		0	4	0	2	6	6	2	2	4	4	6	0	1	1	1	21
20	Murray Williams		2	2	0	0	0	0	0	2	2	1	4	0	1	1	2	11
42	Toraino Walker		0	0	0	0	1	2	0	1	1	0	1	0	0	0	0	4
21	Steve Pikiell		0	0	0	0	0	0	0	0	0	0	0	0	0	0	0	1
31	Tim Pikiell		0	0	0	0	0	0	0	0	0	0	0	0	0	0	0	1
30	Marc Suhr		1	1	0	0	0	0	0	0	0	0	2	0	0	0	0	1
11	Oliver Macklin		0	0	0	0	0	0	0	0	0	0	0	0	0	0	0	1
	TEAM REBOUNDS (included in Totals)								1	2	3							
	TOTALS		27	53	3	10	38	44	10	22	32	26	95	9	14	3	11	200

TOTAL FG %: 1st Half 13-24 54.2   2nd Half 14-29 48.3   Game 27-53 50.9   Deadball
3-Pt. FG %: 1st Half 1-4 25.0   2nd Half 2-6 33.3   Game 3-10 30.0   Rebounds 3
FT%: 1st Half 21-34 91.3   2nd Half 17-21 81.0   Game 38-44 86.4

HOME Boston College

No.	Player Name		FG	FGA	FG	FGA	FT	FTA	Off	Def	Tot	PF	TP	A	TO	BLK	S	MIN
			Total FG		**3-point**				**Rebounds**									
14	Lior Arditti	f	2	8	1	5	8	9	0	2	2	6	13	1	3	0	1	30
15	Bryan Edwards	f	3	6	2	4	5	7	1	2	3	2	13	4	3	0	3	34
23	Michael Reese	c	5	13	0	2	1	2	4	4	8	4	11	4	2	1	0	32
35	Doug Able	g	9	12	0	0	3	7	2	5	7	2	21	1	6	0	1	36
44	David Hinton	g	2	5	0	1	2	2	0	0	0	3	6	1	5	0	1	25
40	Reggie Pruitt		1	1	0	0	0	0	0	1	1	0	2	0	0	0	0	4
22	Corey Jackson		1	1	0	0	2	2	1	1	2	5	4	1	1	0	0	9
30	Bobby Moran		1	2	0	1	0	0	0	2	2	4	2	2	2	0	0	10
31	Corey Beasley		1	3	0	0	0	1	2	0	2	3	2	0	1	0	0	15
32	Walter Lundy		0	1	0	1	0	0	0	0	0	0	0	0	0	0	0	1
11	Bobby Ray Smith		0	0	0	0	0	0	0	0	0	0	0	0	1	0	0	2
55	Daryl Michals		0	1	0	0	0	0	1	0	1	0	0	0	0	0	0	2
	TEAM REBOUNDS (included in Totals)								2	2	4							
	TOTALS		25	53	3	14	21	30	13	19	32	29	74	14	24	1	6	200

TOTAL FG %: 1st Half 16-30 53.3   2nd Half 9-23 39.1   Game 25-53 47.2   Deadball
3-Pt. FG %: 1st Half 2-7 28.6   2nd Half 1-7 14.3   Game 3-14 21.4   Rebounds 2
FT%: 1st Half 4-8 50.0   2nd Half 17-22 77.3   Game 21-30 70.0

OFFICIALS: Jim Burr, Tim Higgins, Gene Monje
Technical Fouls: UConn Burrell
Attendance 8,604 (Sellout)

SCORE BY PERIODS	1st H.	2nd H.	OT	OT	FINAL
Connecticut	48	47	—	—	95
Boston College	38	36	—	—	74

VISITORS Seton Hall

No.	Player Name		FG	FGA	FG	FGA	FT	FTA	Off	Def	Tot	PF	TP	A	TO	BLK	S	MIN
31	Michael Cooper	f	4	10	0	0	0	0	4	3	7	6	8	1	6	1	0	36
30	Frantz Volcy	f	3	9	0	0	4	5	0	5	5	5	10	0	3	3	0	38
32	Anthony Avent	c	1	2	0	0	0	1	1	7	8	5	2	2	2	1	0	24
24	Terry Dehere	g	4	10	3	6	9	10	0	3	3	3	20	2	2	1	1	29
20	Oliver Taylor	g	5	15	2	4	0	0	2	0	2	5	12	3	4	0	1	27
22	Gordon Winchester		1	2	0	0	1	2	0	4	4	2	3	1	2	1	2	17
33	Marco Lokar		1	2	1	2	0	0	0	0	0	3	3	1	3	0	1	13
13	Daryl Crist		0	1	0	1	0	0	0	1	1	3	0	1	2	0	0	10
29	Jim Dickinson		0	0	0	0	0	0	0	0	0	0	0	1	0	0	0	1
14	Jose Rebimbas		0	0	0	0	0	0	0	0	0	0	0	0	0	0	0	2
4	Kerry Kestion		0	1	0	0	0	0	1	0	1	0	0	0	0	0	0	1
21	Michael Murphy		0	0	0	0	0	0	0	0	0	0	0	0	0	0	0	1
10	Lonny Evans		0	0	0	0	0	0	0	0	0	0	0	0	0	0	0	1
	TEAM REBOUNDS (included in Totals)								5	2	7							
	TOTALS		19	52	6	13	14	18	13	25	38	32	58	12	24	7	5	200

TOTAL FG %:   1st Half 40.9   2nd Half 33.3   Game 19-52 36.5   Deadball
3-Pt. FG %:   1st Half 65.7   2nd Half 40.0   Game 6-13 46.2   Rebounds 1
FT%:   1st Half 66.7   2nd Half 88.9   Game 14-18 77.8

HOME Connecticut

No.	Player Name		FG	FGA	FG	FGA	FT	FTA	Off	Def	Tot	PF	TP	A	TO	BLK	S	MIN
24	Scott Burrell	f	1	4	0	0	4	6	2	3	5	2	6	0	1	0	3	30
40	Nadav Henefeld	f	2	7	0	2	6	6	1	2	3	2	10	5	3	0	5	32
22	Rod Sellers	c	2	7	0	0	8	10	1	4	5	3	9	0	1	1	0	26
32	Tate George	g	7	9	0	0	6	8	0	4	4	3	20	4	2	0	6	34
13	Chris Smith	g	4	13	0	1	5	8	1	2	3	4	16	1	3	0	2	34
42	Toraino Walker		1	2	0	0	0	0	1	3	4	2	2	0	0	0	0	6
20	Murray Williams		1	2	0	0	2	4	1	1	2	4	4	0	1	0	0	9
15	John Gwynn		3	5	1	1	0	0	0	1	1	0	7	1	0	0	1	12
23	Lyman DePriest		1	3	0	0	0	1	2	1	3	0	2	0	1	0	0	6
55	Dan Cyrulik		0	0	0	0	0	0	0	0	0	1	0	1	0	0	0	1
11	Oliver Macklin		0	0	0	0	0	0	1	0	1	0	0	0	0	0	0	1
30	Marc Suhr		0	1	0	0	0	0	0	0	0	0	0	0	0	0	0	1
31	Tim Pikiell		0	0	0	0	0	0	0	0	0	0	0	0	0	0	0	1
21	Steve Pikiell		0	0	0	0	0	0	0	0	0	0	0	0	0	0	0	1
	TEAM REBOUNDS (included in Totals)								3	2	5							
	TOTALS		22	53	1	4	31	43	13	23	36	21	76	12	12	1	17	200

TOTAL FG %:   1st Half 37.9   2nd Half 45.8   Game 22-53 41.5   Deadball
3-Pt. FG %:   1st Half 0.0   2nd Half 100.0   Game 1-4 25.0   Rebounds 5
FT%:   1st Half 77.6   2nd Half 68.0   Game 31-43 72.1

OFFICIALS: Jim Burr, Larry Lembo, Bob Donato
Technical Fouls: None
Attendance 16,212 (Sellout)

SCORE BY PERIODS	1st H.	2nd H.	OT	OT	FINAL
Seton Hall	26	32	—	—	58
Connecticut	36	40	—	—	76

1990 Big East Tournament—Semi-Finals

VISITORS Georgetown

Date March 10, 1990   **Site** Madison Square Garden, NY

No.	Player Name		Total FG FG	Total FG FGA	3-point FG	3-point FGA	FT	FTA	Rebounds Off	Rebounds Def	Rebounds Tot	PF	TP	A	TO	BLK	S	MIN
24	Anthony Allen	f	1	1	0	0	0	0	1	0	1	0	2	0	2	0	0	2
33	Alonzo Mourning	f	4	7	0	0	4	8	4	6	10	5	12	2	3	1	0	33
55	Dikembe Mutombo	c	3	3	0	0	0	0	2	5	7	4	4	0	2	2	1	26
12	Dwayne Bryant	g	2	5	2	4	0	1	1	0	1	4	6	9	4	0	1	39
20	Mark Tillmon	g	8	21	4	6	3	5	3	4	7	4	23	0	6	0	1	35
50	Sam Jefferson		0	3	0	0	3	4	2	3	5	2	3	0	0	0	0	27
41	Antoine Stoudamire		3	10	2	8	0	0	0	2	2	4	8	0	1	0	0	20
11	David Edwards		1	2	0	1	0	0	0	0	0	0	2	2	1	0	0	11
30	Ronny Thompson		0	1	0	0	0	0	0	0	0	0	0	0	0	0	0	7
	TEAM REBOUNDS (included in Totals)								6	5	11							
	TOTALS		21	53	8	19	10	18	19	25	44	23	60	13	19	3	3	200

TOTAL FG %: 1st Half 59.1   2nd Half 25.8   Game 21-53 39.6   Deadball
3-Pt. FG %: 1st Half 57.1   2nd Half 33.3   Game 8-19 42.1   Rebounds 1
FT%: 1st Half 75.0   2nd Half 40.0   Game 10-18 55.6

HOME Connecticut

No.	Player Name		Total FG FG	Total FG FGA	3-point FG	3-point FGA	FT	FTA	Rebounds Off	Rebounds Def	Rebounds Tot	PF	TP	A	TO	BLK	S	MIN
24	Scott Burrell	f	2	8	0	1	4	6	2	2	4	2	8	3	1	1	2	32
40	Nadav Henefeld	f	4	8	0	1	1	3	3	3	6	5	9	1	3	2	2	31
22	Rod Sellers	c	0	0	0	0	0	0	0	0	0	1	0	0	0	0	0	2
32	Tate George	g	4	12	1	3	0	0	4	0	4	3	9	3	1	0	1	27
13	Chris Smith	g	6	11	3	4	3	3	0	2	2	1	18	4	0	0	2	37
55	Dan Cyrulik		3	9	0	0	0	1	5	2	7	2	6	0	1	1	1	21
20	Murray Williams		1	2	0	0	0	0	0	1	1	2	2	1	1	0	0	14
42	Toraino Walker		2	3	0	0	0	1	1	5	6	2	4	0	0	0	1	17
15	John Gwynn		2	6	2	3	3	4	0	1	1	1	9	2	1	0	1	13
23	Lyman DePriest		0	0	0	0	0	0	0	0	0	0	0	0	0	0	0	2
11	Oliver Macklin		0	0	0	0	0	0	0	0	0	0	0	0	0	0	0	1
21	Steve Pikiell		0	0	0	0	0	0	0	0	0	0	0	0	0	0	0	1
30	Marc Suhr		0	0	0	0	0	0	0	0	0	0	0	0	0	0	0	1
31	Tim Pikiell		0	0	0	0	0	0	0	0	0	0	0	0	0	0	0	1
	TEAM REBOUNDS (included in Totals)								2	4	6							
	TOTALS		24	59	6	12	11	18	17	20	37	19	65	14	8	4	10	200

TOTAL FG %: 1st Half 38.2   2nd Half 44.0   Game 24-59 40.7   Deadball
3-Pt. FG %: 1st Half 37.5   2nd Half 75.0   Game 6-12 50.0   Rebounds 0
FT%: 1st Half 20.0   2nd Half 76.9   Game 11-18 61.1

OFFICIALS: Pete Pavis, Gene Monje, Mickey Crowley
Technical Fouls: None
Attendance 18,212 (Sellout)

SCORE BY PERIODS	1st H.	2nd H.	OT	OT	FINAL
Georgetown	36	24	—	—	60
Connecticut	30	35	—	—	65

1990 Big East Tournament—Championship Game
Date March 11, 1990 **Site** Madison Square Garden, NY

VISITORS Connecticut

No.	Player Name		Total FG FG	Total FG FGA	3-point FG	3-point FGA	FT	FTA	Rebounds Off	Rebounds Def	Rebounds Tot	PF	TP	A	TO	BLK	S	MIN
24	Scott Burrell	f	0	4	0	1	1	2	1	3	4	3	1	3	2	1	1	23
40	Nadav Henefeld	f	2	7	0	2	0	0	0	3	3	4	4	1	2	0	3	34
55	Dan Cyrulik	c	0	3	0	0	0	0	2	0	2	2	0	0	2	1	1	14
13	Chris Smith	g	7	16	2	3	4	5	1	1	2	2	20	2	1	0	0	37
32	Tate George	g	7	11	0	0	8	8	2	0	2	3	22	3	2	0	2	31
15	John Gwynn		6	7	1	2	3	4	1	1	2	0	16	0	0	0	0	12
20	Murray Williams		0	3	0	0	0	0	0	0	0	2	0	0	2	1	1	14
22	Rod Sellers		0	0	0	0	0	0	0	0	0	0	0	0	0	0	0	2
42	Toraino Walker		3	4	0	0	5	7	2	4	6	4	11	1	0	0	4	24
23	Lyman DePriest		2	2	0	0	0	0	2	0	2	2	4	3	2	0	1	9
	TEAM REBOUNDS (included in Totals)								1	5	6							
	TOTALS		27	57	3	8	21	26	12	17	29	22	78	13	13	3	13	200

TOTAL FG %:   1st Half 48.5   2nd Half 45.8   Game 27-57 47.4   Deadball
3-Pt. FG %:   1st Half 25.0   2nd Half 50.0   Game 3-8   37.5   Rebounds 2
FT%:   1st Half 90.0   2nd Half 75.0   Game 21-26 80.8

HOME Syracuse

No.	Player Name		Total FG FG	Total FG FGA	3-point FG	3-point FGA	FT	FTA	Rebounds Off	Rebounds Def	Rebounds Tot	PF	TP	A	TO	BLK	S	MIN
44	Derrick Coleman	f	4	5	0	0	5	6	2	8	10	4	13	6	3	0	0	38
38	Billy Owens	f	5	11	1	2	2	4	4	3	7	4	13	8	4	0	1	39
23	LeRon Ellis	c	1	3	0	0	0	2	1	2	3	1	2	0	1	0	0	12
12	Michael Edwards	g	1	4	1	4	0	0	0	1	1	2	3	2	5	0	0	25
32	Stevie Thompson	g	10	14	0	1	1	3	2	5	7	5	21	1	3	0	0	39
40	Tony Scott		4	6	3	5	1	2	0	1	1	3	12	0	1	1	0	19
34	Richard Manning		1	3	0	0	0	1	1	0	1	0	2	0	0	0	0	6
23	David Johnson		3	5	1	2	2	4	0	0	0	3	9	1	3	0	1	21
33	Mike Hopkins		0	0	0	0	0	0	0	0	0	0	0	1	0	0	0	2
	TEAM REBOUNDS (included in Totals)								2	1	3							
	TOTALS		29	51	6	14	11	22	12	21	33	22	75	19	20	1	2	200

TOTAL FG %:   1st Half 53.8   2nd Half 60.0   Game 29-51 56.9   Deadball
3-Pt. FG %:   1st Half 40.0   2nd Half 44.4   Game 6-14   42.9   Rebounds 4
FT%:   1st Half 38.5   2nd Half 66.7   Game 11-22 50.0

OFFICIALS: Jim Howell, Larry Lembo, Jodi Sylvester
Technical Fouls: None
Attendance 18,212 (Sellout)

SCORE BY PERIODS	1st H.	2nd H.	OT	OT	FINAL
Connecticut	42	36	—	—	78
Syracuse	35	40	—	—	75

1990 NCAA Men's Basketball Championship—First Round

VISITORS Boston University
Date March 15, 1990 **Site** Hartford CC, Hartford, CT

No.	Player Name		Total FG FG	Total FG FGA	3-point FG	3-point FGA	FT	FTA	Reb Off	Reb Def	Reb Tot	PF	TP	A	TO	BLK	S	MIN
31	David King	f	0	2	0	0	0	0	0	1	1	1	0	1	2	0	0	6
32	Bill Brigham	f	2	3	0	0	0	0	3	5	8	5	4	0	6	1	0	29
00	Ron Moses	c	5	9	0	0	0	0	0	8	8	2	10	0	4	2	1	33
4	Mark Daly	g	1	4	1	2	0	0	0	2	2	3	3	2	3	0	0	25
15	Steven Key	g	7	12	3	3	0	0	0	1	1	2	17	6	4	0	2	37
34	Fred Davy		3	11	0	0	2	5	5	5	10	3	8	2	3	0	1	31
14	Reggie Stewart		2	8	0	2	2	2	1	1	2	0	6	2	3	0	0	21
42	Jason Scott		1	1	0	0	0	0	0	1	1	2	2	0	2	0	0	13
41	Scott White		0	0	0	0	0	0	0	0	0	0	0	0	0	0	0	3
10	Adam Olmsted		0	0	0	0	0	1	0	0	0	0	0	0	0	0	0	1
24	Francis Kalitsi		1	1	0	0	0	0	1	0	1	0	2	0	0	0	0	1
	TEAM REBOUNDS (included in Totals)								0	3	3							
	TOTALS		22	51	4	7	4	8	10	27	37	18	52	13	27	3	4	200

TOTAL FG %: 1st Half 12-28 42.9 2nd Half 10-23 43.5 Game 22-51 43.1 Deadball
3-Pt. FG %: 1st Half 3-3 100.0 2nd Half 1-4 25.0 Game 4-7 57.1 Rebounds 1
FT%: 1st Half 1-2 50.0 2nd Half 3-6 50.0 Game 4-8 50.0

HOME Connecticut

No.	Player Name		Total FG FG	Total FG FGA	3-point FG	3-point FGA	FT	FTA	Reb Off	Reb Def	Reb Tot	PF	TP	A	TO	BLK	S	MIN
24	Scott Burrell	f	2	6	0	0	5	7	4	3	7	2	9	1	1	1	4	28
40	Nadav Henefeld	f	7	16	1	3	4	5	4	3	7	2	19	2	0	0	3	28
22	Rod Sellers	c	2	3	0	0	0	0	2	5	7	2	4	0	1	0	1	20
13	Chris Smith	g	5	17	4	7	5	6	3	1	4	2	19	3	3	0	3	29
32	Tate George	g	4	10	0	2	1	3	1	2	3	0	9	5	2	1	4	37
20	Murray Williams		0	0	0	0	0	0	0	1	1	0	0	0	0	0	0	5
15	John Gwynn		5	12	0	1	0	2	1	1	2	1	10	0	2	0	1	19
42	Toraino Walker		1	3	0	0	2	2	3	2	5	2	4	0	0	0	1	15
55	Dan Cyrulik		0	0	0	0	0	0	0	0	0	0	0	0	0	0	0	4
23	Lyman DePriest		1	2	0	0	0	1	1	2	3	1	2	1	1	0	2	14
22	Steve Pikiell		0	0	0	0	0	0	0	0	0	0	0	0	1	0	0	1
	TEAM REBOUNDS (included in Totals)								3	2	5							
	TOTALS		27	69	5	13	17	26	22	22	44	12	76	12	11	2	19	200

TOTAL FG %: 1st Half 9-30 30.0 2nd Half 18-39 46.2 Game 27-69 39.1 Deadball
3-Pt. FG %: 1st Half 2-5 40.0 2nd Half 3-8 37.5 Game 5-13 38.1 Rebounds 2
FT%: 1st Half 9-17 52.9 2nd Half 8-9 88.9 Game 17-26 65.4

OFFICIALS: David Hall, Gary Petro, Gerald Boudreaux
Technical Fouls: None
Attendance 15,937 (Sellout)

SCORE BY PERIODS	1st H.	2nd H.	OT	OT	FINAL
Boston Univ.	28	24	—	—	52
Connecticut	29	47	—	—	76

1990 NCAA Men's Basketball Championship—Second Round

VISITORS California

Date March 17, 1990 **Site** Hartford CC, Hartford, CT

No.	Player Name		Total FG FG	Total FG FGA	3-point FG	3-point FGA	FT	FTA	Rebounds Off	Rebounds Def	Rebounds Tot	PF	TP	A	TO	BLK	S	MIN
38	Bryant Walton	f	3	7	1	4	0	0	0	8	8	4	7	0	4	0	0	32
40	Roy Fisher	f	6	7	0	1	5	8	1	5	6	3	17	2	10	1	0	39
15	Brian Hendrick	c	5	7	0	0	2	4	1	5	6	4	12	0	5	1	1	35
21	Keith Smith	g	3	6	0	0	3	3	0	3	3	3	9	5	7	0	0	37
24	Ryan Drew	g	2	6	1	4	0	2	1	1	2	0	5	2	0	0	0	23
23	Bill Elleby		0	4	0	2	2	2	0	0	0	1	2	0	1	0	1	18
34	Andre Reyes		0	0	0	0	0	0	0	0	0	0	0	1	0	0	0	4
14	Sean Harrell		0	1	0	0	2	3	1	0	1	3	2	1	1	1	0	8
3	Eric McDonough		0	0	0	0	0	0	0	0	0	0	0	0	0	0	0	1
22	John Carty		0	0	0	0	0	0	0	0	0	0	0	0	0	0	0	1
35	Rich Branham		0	1	0	1	0	0	0	0	0	0	0	0	0	0	0	1
41	Andrew Brigham		0	0	0	0	0	0	0	0	0	1	0	0	0	0	0	1
	TEAM REBOUNDS (included in Totals)								3	4	7							
	TOTALS		19	39	2	12	14	22	7	26	33	19	54	11	28	3	2	200

TOTAL FG %: 1st Half 9-21 47.9   2nd Half 10-18 55.6   Game 19-39 48.7   Deadball
3-Pt. FG %: 1st Half 2-10 20.0   2nd Half 0-2 00.0   Game 2-12 16.7   Rebounds 3
FT%: 1st Half 6-11 54.5   2nd Half 8-11 72.7   Game 14-22 63.6

HOME Connecticut

No.	Player Name		Total FG FG	Total FG FGA	3-point FG	3-point FGA	FT	FTA	Rebounds Off	Rebounds Def	Rebounds Tot	PF	TP	A	TO	BLK	S	MIN
24	Scott Burrell	f	4	9	0	0	5	6	5	2	7	3	13	2	1	0	1	31
40	Nadav Henefeld	f	4	7	1	1	1	2	0	3	3	3	10	2	1	0	4	30
22	Rod Sellers	c	1	4	0	0	0	0	2	1	3	2	2	1	1	0	1	14
13	Chris Smith	g	6	17	5	13	7	8	1	2	3	2	24	2	3	0	2	33
32	Tate George	g	4	9	0	1	2	2	1	2	3	2	10	3	2	0	3	35
42	Toraino Walker		1	1	0	0	0	0	1	2	3	3	2	1	0	0	0	13
20	Murray Williams		0	1	0	0	0	0	0	0	0	0	0	0	2	0	0	7
15	John Gwynn		3	10	1	2	2	3	1	3	4	1	9	0	0	0	1	15
23	Lyman DePriest		1	4	0	0	1	2	1	2	3	3	3	0	1	0	4	18
55	Dan Cyrulik		0	0	0	0	0	0	0	0	0	2	0	0	0	0	0	2
21	Steve Pikiell		0	0	0	0	1	2	0	0	0	0	1	0	0	0	0	1
11	Oliver Macklin		0	1	0	0	0	0	0	0	0	0	0	0	0	0	0	1
	TEAM REBOUNDS (included in Totals)								3	0	3							
	TOTALS		24	63	7	17	19	25	15	17	32	21	74	11	11	0	16	200

TOTAL FG %: 1st Half 14-32 43.8   2nd Half 10-31 32.3   Game 24-63 38.1   Deadball
3-Pt. FG %: 1st Half 5-13 38.5   2nd Half 2-4 50.0   Game 7-17 41.2   Rebounds 5
FT%: 1st Half 9-11 81.3   2nd Half 10-14 71.4   Game 19-25 76.0

OFFICIALS: Paul Hausman, Scott Thornly, Larry Rose
Technical Fouls: California Bench
Attendance 16,011 (Sellout)

SCORE BY PERIODS	1st H.	2nd H.	OT	OT	FINAL
California	26	28	—	—	54
Connecticut	42	32	—	—	74

VISITORS Clemson

1990 NCAA Men's Basketball Championship—Regional Semifinal
Date March 22, 1990   **Site** Meadowlands, East Rutherford, NJ

No.	Player Name		FG	FGA	FG	FGA	FT	FTA	Off	Def	Tot	PF	TP	A	TO	BLK	S	MIN
22	Sean Tyson	f	5	8	0	0	1	3	2	2	4	0	11	2	2	0	2	22
34	Dale Davis	f	6	10	0	0	3	5	7	10	17	2	15	0	3	1	0	37
41	Elden Campbell	c	5	11	0	0	5	7	2	6	8	3	15	1	5	3	1	33
12	Marion Cash	g	2	9	1	1	3	5	2	1	3	3	8	4	1	0	2	33
13	Derrick Forrest	g	2	4	0	2	2	2	0	1	1	1	6	2	3	0	2	27
04	Kirkland Howling		2	8	1	6	2	3	0	1	1	2	7	1	0	0	0	24
11	David Young		1	2	1	2	0	0	1	0	1	1	3	0	3	0	2	9
15	Shawn Lastinger		1	2	1	1	0	0	0	1	1	1	3	1	0	0	0	4
25	Ricky Jones		0	0	0	0	0	0	0	0	0	1	0	0	0	0	0	2
42	Wayne Buckingham		1	2	0	0	0	0	1	1	2	2	2	0	0	0	0	8
44	Colby Brown		0	0	0	0	0	0	0	0	0	0	0	0	0	0	0	1
	TEAM REBOUNDS (included in Totals)								2	0	2							
	TOTALS		25	56	4	12	16	25	17	23	40	16	70	11	20	4	9	200

TOTAL FG %:   1st Half 36.0   2nd Half 51.6   Game 25-56 44.6   Deadball
3-Pt. FG %:   1st Half 25.0   2nd Half 37.5   Game 4-12 33.3   Rebounds 0
FT%:   1st Half 71.4   2nd Half 54.5   Game 16-25 64.0

HOME Connecticut

No.	Player Name		FG	FGA	FG	FGA	FT	FTA	Off	Def	Tot	PF	TP	A	TO	BLK	S	MIN
24	Scott Burrell	f	2	9	0	0	5	6	6	9	15	3	9	1	1	0	2	32
40	Nadav Henefeld	f	1	3	0	1	0	0	0	3	3	4	2	3	4	0	0	22
42	Toraino Walker	c	1	2	0	0	0	0	0	2	2	4	2	0	5	0	1	14
13	Chris Smith	g	8	14	4	6	3	3	2	1	3	2	23	5	3	0	1	33
32	Tate George	g	5	12	0	1	2	2	0	1	1	2	12	4	1	1	1	30
15	John Gwynn		4	13	0	2	1	2	1	0	1	1	9	0	3	0	0	17
20	Murray Williams		0	1	0	0	0	0	0	0	0	2	0	1	0	0	0	10
22	Rod Sellers		2	3	0	0	0	1	2	1	3	1	4	0	0	0	0	19
23	Lyman DePriest		4	6	0	0	0	0	2	0	2	2	8	2	1	0	1	17
55	Dan Cyrulik		1	1	0	0	0	1	0	0	0	2	2	0	1	0	1	6
	TEAM REBOUNDS (included in Totals)								3	3	6							
	TOTALS		28	64	4	10	11	15	16	20	36	23	71	16	19	1	7	200

TOTAL FG %:   1st Half 40.0   2nd Half 50.0   Game 28-64 43.8   Deadball
3-Pt. FG %:   1st Half 28.6   2nd Half 66.7   Game 4-10 40.0   Rebounds 0
FT%:   1st Half 66.7   2nd Half 77.8   Game 11-15 73.3

OFFICIALS: Jim Bain, Jim Stupin, David Bair
Technical Fouls: Davis-Clemson
Attendance 19,546

SCORE BY PERIODS	1st H.	2nd H.	OT	OT	FINAL
Clemson	29	41	—	—	70
Connecticut	38	33	—	—	71

1990 NCAA Men's Basketball Championship—Regional Final
Date March 24, 1990   **Site** Meadowlands, East Rutherford, NJ

VISITORS Duke

No.	Player Name		FG	FGA	FG	FGA	FT	FTA	Off	Def	Tot	PF	TP	A	TO	BLK	S	MIN
			Total FG		**3-point**				**Rebounds**									
21	Robert Brickey	f	1	4	0	0	0	0	1	0	1	2	2	1	4	0	1	14
32	Christian Laettner	f	7	8	0	0	9	11	1	4	5	3	23	2	1	1	2	38
30	Alaa Abdelnaby	c	9	16	0	0	9	12	5	9	14	2	27	0	1	2	1	37
03	Phil Henderson	g	7	20	4	10	3	3	0	3	3	2	21	1	1	0	0	42
11	Bobby Hurley	g	0	9	0	2	3	4	0	2	2	3	3	8	2	0	4	43
05	Bill McCaffrey		0	2	0	0	1	2	0	1	1	0	1	1	1	0	0	5
22	Greg Koubek		0	1	0	1	0	0	1	1	2	0	0	0	1	0	0	6
23	Brian Davis		1	2	0	0	0	0	1	2	3	4	2	1	1	0	1	23
25	Thomas Hill		0	2	0	0	0	0	1	2	3	0	0	1	0	0	0	17
	TEAM REBOUNDS (included in Totals)								2	0	2							
	TOTALS		25	64	4	13	25	32	12	24	36	16	79	15	12	3	9	225

TOTAL FG %: 1st Half 40.6   2nd Half 34.6   Game 25-64 39.1   Deadball
3-Pt. FG %: 1st Half 28.6   2nd Half 20.0   Game 4-13 30.8   Rebounds 2
FT%:   1st Half 81.8   2nd Half 76.2   Game 25-32 78.1

HOME Connecticut

No.	Player Name		FG	FGA	FG	FGA	FT	FTA	Off	Def	Tot	PF	TP	A	TO	BLK	S	MIN
			Total FG		**3-point**				**Rebounds**									
24	Scott Burrell	f	6	10	0	0	0	0	4	1	5	5	12	1	1	0	1	22
40	Nadav Henefeld	f	5	10	1	4	4	4	2	4	6	3	15	4	4	1	1	44
22	Rod Sellers	c	0	1	0	0	1	2	0	5	5	3	1	0	1	4	0	24
13	Chris Smith	g	4	16	1	4	2	2	0	4	4	1	11	5	7	0	2	42
32	Tate George	g	4	8	1	2	0	0	0	2	2	4	9	4	0	0	0	27
15	John Gwynn		6	15	0	4	3	3	0	4	4	3	15	1	2	0	0	28
20	Murray Williams		0	0	0	0	0	0	0	0	0	0	0	0	0	0	0	1
23	Lyman DePriest		1	1	0	0	0	0	1	2	3	4	2	0	3	0	1	11
42	Toraino Walker		4	5	0	0	1	1	3	2	5	3	9	1	1	1	1	21
55	Dan Cyrulik		2	2	0	0	0	0	1	0	1	0	4	0	0	0	0	5
	TEAM REBOUNDS (included in Totals)								2	8	10							
	TOTALS		32	68	3	14	11	12	13	32	45	26	78	16	19	6	6	225

TOTAL FG %: 1st Half 41.9   2nd Half 56.7   Game 32-68 47.1   Deadball
3-Pt. FG %: 1st Half 0.0   2nd Half 33.3   Game 3-14 21.4   Rebounds 0
FT%:   1st Half 80.0   2nd Half 100.0   Game 11-12 91.7

OFFICIALS: Ed Hightower, Gordon Birk, David Hall
Technical Fouls: None
Attendance 19,546

SCORE BY PERIODS	1st H.	2nd H.	OT	OT	FINAL
Duke	37	35	7	—	79
Connecticut	30	42	6	—	78